D0220255

Careers Guidance in Context

Careers Guidance in Context

Bill Gothard, Phil Mignot, Marcus Offer and
Melvyn Ruff

SAGE Publications
London • Thousand Oaks • New Delhi

SAGE Publications Ltd
6 Bohhill Street
London EC2A 4PU

SAGE Publications Inc
2455 Teller Road
Thousand Oaks, California 91320

SAGE Publications India Pvt Ltd
32, M-Block Market
Greater Kailash – I
New Delhi 110 048

British Library Cataloguing in Publication data
A catalogue record for this book is
available from the British Library

ISBN 0 7619 6905 5
ISBN 0 7619 6906 3 (pbk)

Library of Congress Control Nmber: available

Typeset by Keystroke, Jacaranda Lodge, Wolverhampton
Printed in Great Britain by Biddles Ltd, Guildford, Surrey

CONTENTS

1

CAREERS GUIDANCE IN A NEW ERA

There is considerable consensus that at the start of a new century we are living in a new era, although how it is described varies. Castells (1999a) calls it the 'information age', Wijers and Meijers (1996) the 'knowledge society', Mulgan (1997) a 'connected world', and Beck (1999) 'risk society'. Although the titles vary, there is a great deal of agreement as to what characterises this new era, and the consequences of the rapid change witnessed in the last 20 years. The impact of this change is being increasingly explored by those writing about careers guidance (Collin and Watts, 1996; Roberts, 1997; Savickas, 1993) and it is the purpose of this chapter to explore the nature of the new era in order to consider the consequences for career guidance services and for its impact on the role of careers workers.

The nature of the new era

In his recent important study, Castells (1999a) discusses the rise of the network society which he describes as based on a new mode of development, informationalism, historically shaped by the restructuring of the capitalist mode of production. What is new about informationalism is that the action of knowledge upon knowledge itself is the main source of productivity, and thus the development of technology is directed towards ever increasing levels of complexity and information processing. Castells claims that this new technology is so pervasive that it penetrates society in such a way that new forms of social interaction, social control and social change are emerging. Indeed, these changes can be identified on a global scale with all societies being influenced by informationalism, to some extent.

Mulgan (1997) calls this 'connexity' and discusses how we live in a connected world. He uses this term rather than information or knowledge because connexity is the capacity to store, to spread, to disseminate and connect that makes sense of information processing and gives value to it. The pervasiveness of the new technology springs from the fact that information is an essential part of all human activity. This leads to networks at many different levels, providing great flexibility and potential for change. Another vital feature of this technological revolution is the highly integrated nature of the technology, leading to powerful connections between tele-communications, computing and electronics. These characteristics have led to the establishment of a truly global economy which is new; it is the capacity to work as a unit in real time on a planetary scale (Castells, 1999a). Thus there are globally integrated financial markets facilitating the rapid flow of capital, whilst science, technology and information are organised on a global scale and markets are increasingly globalised.

The term 'globalisation' is increasingly used as a way of defining this new era, and there has been much debate as to the meaning of the term. Giddens (2000) emphasises four aspects to globalisation: first and most important, the world-wide communications revolution; second, the 'weightless economy' with financial markets leading the way; third, the demise of the Soviet Union; and finally, growing equality between women and men. Davis (1998) describes globalisation as capitalism in the age of electronics, making clear the crucial link between the new technology and the economic system. Hobsbawm (2000) puts a different emphasis on globalisation, describing it as the elimination of technical obstacles rather than economic ones, with an abolition of distance and time. Kundnani (1998) sees the globalised market as based on the use of informational and symbolic goods which are themselves the most dynamic and prof-itable areas, resulting in manufacturing relying for its competitiveness on information processing and leading to a state of perpetual technical innovation in order to remain competitive. Globalisation has also meant an increasing interdependence of international trade and global competition with information technology as the 'indispensable medium for technologies between different segments of the labour force across national bound-aries' (Castells, 1999a). Collin and Watts (1996) describe these dramatic changes as a move to a 'post-industrial stage' or 'post-Fordism', with mass production controlled by a centralised bureaucracy now being replaced by small-batch production using computer technology and a flexible workforce. In addition, there has been a 'crisis' of the large corporation and a growth of small and medium employers. These changes in the economy have led to the growth of the network enterprise (Castells, 1999a) which makes material the culture of the informational/global economy; it trans-forms signals into commodities by processing knowledge.

The consequence of these developments is that work and employment is being radically changed. Post-industrialism is characterised first by an emphasis on information generation as the main source of productivity, second by a shift from goods production to the delivery of services, and finally by the rapid growth of managerial, professional and technical occupations, with increasing polarisation within the occupational structure. Castells (1999a) defines the UK as a service economy model, where manu-facturing employment has rapidly diminished. He sees a new division of labour emerging with occupations clustering around three types of activity:

first, value making, which includes research, design, integration and execution of tasks; second, relation making, which involves networking; and finally, decision making. New terms such as outsourcing, downsizing and customising indicate the trend for a greater degree of individualisation of labour. More people are in temporary and part-time employment; increasing numbers are self-employed so that the traditional form of work, based on full-time employment, clear-cut occupational assignments and a career pattern over the life cycle, is being eroded away (Castells, 1999a).

Mulgan (1997) points out that the new economy lays greater and greater emphasis on exchange and transformation as opposed to direct engagement with materials. He states that it has shifted the centre of gravity of societies away from those occupations which favour continuity on to occupations which favour change, unpredictability, spontaneity, innovation and creativity. The demand is for people with interpersonal and intrapersonal skills to become intermediaries and interpreters dealing with a myriad of human relationships. Increasingly, these skills allow workers to become mobile in the global market. Conversely, those who were in unskilled manufacturing jobs find themselves redundant; this is especially true of men, with women proving to be more adaptable to shifts in the labour market.

This assessment is supported by a number of other writers (Arthur et al., 1999; Collin and Watts, 1996; Killeen, 1996; Roberts, 1997; Savickas, 1993). For example, Arthur et al. (1999) discuss the implications of moving from the 'industrial state' to the 'new economy' for individual workers, claiming that these profound economic changes have led to radical changes in the nature of career. They point to a move from a 'strong' situation that prevailed when large bureaucracies and companies were dominant to a 'weak' situation where work is much more flexible, with, for example, a more feminized workforce balancing home and employment. Killeen (1996) identified a number sources of change that were determining the social context of guidance. These were technological change as exemplified by information technology; globalisation with an internationalisation of careers and products; industrial restructuring and, in particular, the rise of the service sector; unemployment, especially among the young; the rapid increase of women in the labour force; and finally, an ageing labour force. He points to new career realities which imply 'uncertainty, unpredictability, insecurity, reduced likelihood of promotion, increased likelihood of mobility out of one's initial occupation, non-standard contracts and part-time work and self-employment' (1996: 15).

Roberts (1997) talks of prolonged transitions to uncertain destinations facing young people. Prolonged transitions reflect the extent to which young people are either remaining in full-time education post-16 or participating in some training scheme, and the uncertain destinations refer to the rapid economic changes which have transformed the economy, making employment much less predictable. This theme has been further developed by Bentley and Gurumurthy (1999), who discuss changing routes to adulthood brought about by changes in the economic structure and employment and education. They also point to profound differences in family life, in some cases leading to young people becoming homeless; social exclusion, which is concentrated in certain geographical areas, with crime as a particular problem; and increasing mental health problems for young people. Savickas (1993) describes a move from a twentieth-century 'career ethic' based on large bureaucratic organisations, where typically the white middle-class male found success by moving up someone else's ladder, to a twenty-first century 'development ethic', where success comes through cooperation and contribution in a postmodern society in which individuals are more able to shape their lives and meaning is more open to interpretation. Hawkins (1997) suggests a new vocabulary is needed to describe new careers, with terms like portfolio, personal growth, maintaining employability and lifelong learning replacing career, progression, rising income and security and education and training. However, there is also evidence of increasing job insecurity and work intensification (Burchell et al., 1999) especially among professionals, leading to poorer health and greater stress in family relationships.

Social change and identity

Having examined the main economic and technological changes currently taking place, it is appropriate to see how these developments relate to social change and, in particular, to the identities of particular groups such as young people. Gender has been at the heart of social change for the last three decades. Castells (1999b) proclaims the end of patriarchalism – a revolution that goes to the roots of society and to the heart of who we are. This revolution is the result of a number of factors. The new technology which has transformed advanced economies has led to the creation of new jobs, many of which have been filled by women, who have the necessary flexibility and the relational skills demanded. Levinson (1996) divides this paid employment into three categories: unskilled/semi-skilled work offering limited pay and prospects that women often combine with their family responsibilities; traditional 'female occupations' such as teaching and nursing that offer better career prospects but where the most senior posts are often occupied by men; and finally, higher-status occupations in business and the professions where women are increasingly challenging men, but their advancement is sometimes limited. These advances made by women in paid employment are mirrored by higher participation in post-16 education and increasing academic attainment, to the extent that boys are now seen as having problems in attainment.

The change in gender relations is marked in the way in which the concept of the family has altered. The increase in divorce has led to the creation of many one-parent families, mostly headed by women. The 'traditional marriage enterprise' (Kaltreider, 1997; Levinson, 1996) is no longer the norm, with most women having to seek a difficult balance between paid employment, child-rearing and a domestic role. In addition, the concept of the family has been extended to take in gay and lesbian relationships which has further challenged the status quo. Similarly, women's ability to control their fertility has radically increased the choices open to them, leading to later, smaller families or childlessness.

Women's consciousness has been raised by feminist thinking and women's action arising from this new consciousness. Feminism has taken many different forms (Castells, 1999b) that have proved to be pervasive and challenged patriarchal attitudes and institutions. Discrimination and abuse against women still exist but it seems that we are in the middle of a massive experiment to see how much advantage women will take of the egalitarian opportunities now opening up for them. Recent evidence (Bynner et al., 1997) suggests that the benefits for women are seen at the upper end of the educational and occupational scales. With the challenge to the 'patriarchal family' Hage and Powers (1992) propose that new personalities emerge, more complex, less secure, yet more capable of adapting to changing roles in new social contexts.

In regard to young people, Bentley and Gurumurthy (1999) describe the 'new adolescence' as arising earlier than it did a generation ago, but also that the transition to adulthood has become more protracted. They suggest that many of the structures and norms that acted as props and prompts – marriage, childbirth, community structure, employment – have been weakened by wider and more general forms of change. They point to a world where there are opportunities for young people to progress and thrive through individual initiative, but for the disadvantaged minority, the 'new landscape' is threatening and insecure. There is a stark contrast between those young people 'getting on' and those 'getting nowhere' (Bynner et al., 1997).

Increasing attention is being given to this marginalised group of young people. They are at risk for a host of reasons. For instance, many young people live in poor housing in economically run-down areas in which families are workless, possibly with a lone parent. They may have a criminal record or be in care as well as suffering from low esteem, psychosocial disorders and drug abuse. Their educational attainment will be low, based on poor attendance or exclusion, and lacking in work-related skills. This leads to low-paid work or unemployment. Black young people are twice as likely as their white counterparts to belong to this marginalised group (Bentley and Gurumurthy, 1999). Roberts (1997) identifies winners and losers among the young. Winners include girls, some ethnic minority groups and those coming from households with two adults working full-time in good jobs. In their study of young people, Bynner et al. (1997) found a more polarised generation with family background, as expressed by the father's social class, still exercising strong influence on school achievements and occupational positions in adulthood.

The construction of identity has long been of concern to social scientists (Castells, 1999b; Erikson, 1968; Giddens, 1994). Indeed, the issue of 'who we are' and 'who we might become' lies at the heart of careers guidance: thus it is crucial to examine changes brought about by the network society in relation to identity formation. Giddens (1994) maintains that self-identity is not a distinctive trait possessed by the individual. The self emerges as reflexively understood by the person in term of her/his biography. He goes on to draw attention to the diversity of choices offered by 'late modern life' and to the lack of help as to which options should be selected. Choices made help determine lifestyle, which determines not only how to act but who to be.

Lifestyles are determined by pattern of consumption but also by life chances which are strongly conditioned by work, or lack of it. Arthur et al. (1999) describe how in the 'new economy' individuals are able to enact their careers. In this process of enactment, people create their own career narratives as a means of personal sensemaking in a changing environment. The authors maintain that the process creates but also constantly modifies the structures of institutions and of individual lives.

Potentially, a bewildering range of options and choices is available in the network society and so is a great deal of information and expert opinion. Giddens (1994) states that, in this situation, strategic life planning is necessary – life planning being a preparation for future actions mobilised in terms of the self's biography. Actual place become less important with the wide range of options made possible by globalisation and the virtual reality of the net. With each phase of an individual's transition, there tends to be an identity crisis.

There is a debate as to the role played by information technology in this process (Barglow, 1994; Castells, 1999b; Turkle, 1996). Castells (1999b), for example, maintains that because new technology is based on knowledge and information, there is a specially close linkage between culture and productive forces, between spirit and matter, in the informational mode of development. Turkle (1996) explores the relationship people have with computers and the implications of this for their identity. She describes how a culture of simulation substitutes representations of reality for the real, with computer screens the new location for our fantasies. Information technology can lead to a multiplicity of selves, in keeping with the diverse and fluid postmodern world. Whilst recognising the potential benefits of this multiplicity, Barglow (1994) points out the consequence can be insecurity, with less for us to do, perhaps less for us to be – less that establishes us as uniquely human.

The politics of careers guidance

Watts describes careers education and guidance as a profoundly political process, because

It operates at the interface between the individual and society, between self and opportunity, between aspiration and realism. It facilitates the allocation of life chances. Within a society in which such life chances are unequally distributed, it faces the issue of whether it serves to reinforce such inequalities or to reduce them. (1996a: 351)

Thus there is always a political and ideological agenda in relation to careers guidance and this has become increasingly explicit in the 'new economy'.

The growing threat of unemployment, especially amongst young people, that developed during the 1980s thrust careers guidance services into the political arena. The decline in traditional manufacturing industries had led to a sharp reduction in manual occupations, filled mostly by young men. With this radical and painful reshaping of work came a political need to respond to the first large-scale youth unemployment since the 1930s. The 'new right' government of Mrs Thatcher sought to influence careers guidance services in three ways (Watts, 1991). First, from a social control perspective, the government sought to recruit young people onto youth training schemes and report those who turned down places. Second, guidance services were encouraged to attend to the needs of the market by ensuring that market intelligence was excellent and that young people should respond to this accordingly. Finally, it was believed that there should be a market in guidance itself, making it more efficient and more responsive to its client groups.

Governments have had broad aims for guidance services: economic efficiency via their role in the allocation of young people to work, and social equity through access to educational and occupational opportunities (Watts, 1996a). Originally, guidance services in Britain conformed to a social welfare model, being fully funded and controlled by government. With the advent of 'new right' thinking which dominated British political life for nearly two decades, this model has been successfully challenged by a quasi-market model where there are varied sources of funding and control. Thus in 1993, careers guidance services were removed from local government control and put out to tender, resulting in a form of 'privatised' guidance.

With the election of 'New Labour' in 1997, a new emphasis in policy has emerged and this has had a direct impact on the way in which the Careers Service operates. The focus is now upon socially excluded young people, culminating in the publication of 'Bridging the Gap: New Opportunities for 16–18 Year Olds Not in Education, Employment or Training' (SEU, 1999). The Careers Service is now identified as a 'key player in delivering the Department's agenda' (DfEE, 2000a) and will play a major role in the formation of the new youth support service, Connexions, in 2001. Hence, public policy is redefining the Careers Service, this time in conjunction with other agencies such as social work, and creating a new professional role, the personal adviser.

Careers work in higher education has not been immune from the impact of public policy. With the publication of the Dearing Report (National

Commission of Inquiry into Higher Education, 1997), impetus was given to changes that had been taking place during the previous years. Higher education careers services were identified as having a central role in ensuring the employability of their graduates through the introduction of career management skills and transferable skills into the curriculum.

It is clear that careers guidance at all levels will remain central to future governments' policy agendas, because of the emphasis on employability, social inclusion and national targets for education. As a result, the roles occupied by careers staff are changing and the services are being restructured accordingly.

Professional identity and change

As we have seen, those working in careers guidance are also subject to the same forces of change as their clients. Reflecting on this process and becoming more aware of the nature of this change is an essential part of maintaining and developing a credible professional identity. In order to become an effective practitioner, it is important to explore how professional identities are formed. First, training to work in this field involves an element of theory (Kidd et al., 1994) which Brammer (1985) says acts as a rationale for what one does in the name of helping and which involves basic assumptions of how people learn and change their behaviour. Consequently, there are a number of dimensions to this which include values, a cognitive 'map', notions of development, and learning styles.

Second, the practitioner's world view needs to be taken into account (Ivey et al., 1987). By this is meant that we all have a perception of how the world works, how we decide to act, what motivates us and other people, and what are our important values and beliefs. This frame of reference will always influence how practitioners work with clients and thus has to be acknowledged.

Schon (1991), in promoting his notion of the 'reflective practitioner', made a number of points that relate directly to careers staff today. He describes the professional–client relationship as central and contrasts the traditional relationship with that of a new, more reflective relationship. For example, in this new relationship the practitioner has an obligation to make his own understandings accessible to his client and to be ready to explore the client's meanings. It is also significant that the practitioner is more directly accountable to the client.

Schon characterised the reflective practitioner as recognising that s/he is not the only one in the situation to have relevant and important knowledge, that uncertainties may be a source of learning to both parties. By not maintaining a professional façade, a real connection can be made to the client. The relationship can lead to a sense of increased involvement and action. This approach means that a reflective contract allows for mutual respect, a greater sense of partnership, and a shared sense of purpose.

There is a clear recognition of the sorts of issues raised by Schon (1991) and Ivey et al., (1987) in the new learning outcomes for capability in careers guidance (DfEE, 1999). The learning outcomes are set out in seven units and three of them make direct reference to these issues. Unit two, 'Self Evaluation', sets out the need to critically reflect upon and evaluate own practice, and demonstrate commitment to own training, improvement and continuing professional development. Unit five, 'Core Values', focuses on professionalism. Statements are made about students examining and evaluating their own beliefs and values and their effect on the conduct of guidance practice, demonstrating an impartial client-centred approach and developing a critical awareness of potential conflict between agency and professional values. Finally, unit six, 'Equal Opportunities', emphasises the need to develop strategies to identify and manage the effects of own values and beliefs in guidance practice. These new learning outcomes are much more explicit than earlier ones in emphasising the necessity for careers professionals to be reflective practitioners.

2

CAREER DEVELOPMENT THEORY

The way in which our careers develop is a complex process involving many different and changing factors. In order to understand it more clearly, a body of theory is required and this has become increasingly available over the last 100 years. These theories have to be seen within the context of the time they were developed, for as Law (1996a) observed, they have 'responded to the social concerns prevalent' at a particular time. It is necessary to view career development theories as 'growing out of their times' but also influencing the way in which careers guidance has been practised.

Careers guidance formally began with Frank Parsons, who established the Vocation Bureau in Boston (USA) in 1908. The following year he put his ideas into words. First, he stressed, a clear understanding of the individual's aptitudes, interests and limitations was necessary. Second, a knowledge of the requirements and conditions of different kinds of employment was essential. Finally, an ability to match these two would result in successful guidance.

Thus Parsons laid the basis for the notion of talent matching. He went on to suggest some techniques, beginning with the collection of personal data by means of a private interview at some length. Various tests of sight and hearing might well be used, as well as an assessment of memory and general intelligence. He was also concerned with character analysis during the interview. Parsons saw it as part of his work to advise interviewees on the value of voice culture and the economic value of the smile, and he held that if a boy's manners were in any way objectionable or underdeveloped, he should be frankly told and urged to correct his errors.

Occupational information was the basis of his second area of interest and he collected this for use with clients. He advised that a boy who was underdeveloped and inexperienced and showed no special aptitudes should read about occupations and visit places of work and, if feasible, try his hand at different kinds of work.

Frank Parsons does not seem to have been much influenced by the psychological thinking of the time. However, industrial psychologists were becoming increasingly interested in this field, an interest that was stimulated by the First World War. In a sense, this is where the earliest British interest in vocational guidance arises. Cyril Burt joined C.S. Myers at the newly founded National Institute of Industrial Psychology (NIIP) in 1921 and initiated a programme of research which later involved Alec Rodger and carried on until the Second World War. This research focused on the usefulness of psychometric information in guidance and on the need for clearer and more extensive knowledge of occupations. Despite the work of the NIIP, the Juvenile Employment Service did not readily take to psychological testing. Indeed, Birmingham was the only education authority that became extensively involved, and in 1944 it published a report stating that the adoption of scientific methods in vocational guidance improved considerably the advice that can be given to children leaving school.

Person–environment fit theories

Trait and factor

Differential psychology is concerned with the examination of individual differences in terms of traits and factors. In the United States, the leading proponents of this approach were D.G. Patterson and E.G. Williamson, both of the University of Minnesota. Whilst Patterson worked in the Employment Stabilization Research Institute, developing various aptitude tests for use in vocational guidance, it was Williamson (1939) who promoted the trait and factor theory and helped to establish its widespread practice.

The theory is based on the following premises:

1 Individuals are organised in terms of a unique pattern of capabilities and potentialities (traits).
2 These traits are correlated with the requirements of different jobs.
3 Testing is the best means of predicting future job success.
4 Each individual attempts to identify their own traits in order to find a way of working and living which will enable them to use their capabilities effectively.

Williamson laid great emphasis on the individual as a rational being who, once possessing adequate information about themselves, is then capable of making a wise choice. The counsellor uses a selection of tests and other devices to help the client to put aptitudes, interests and personality into some sort of occupational context. Alec Rodger (1952) developed a trait and factor working framework, the seven-point plan, which became widely adopted in the UK. The plan stated that those engaged in vocational guidance need to assemble a profile of information for each individual based on the following seven areas:

1 physical makeup
2 attainments
3 general intelligence
4 special aptitudes
5 interests
6 disposition
7 circumstances.

The seven-point plan bears closer examination as it enshrines much of the trait and factor theory and has played an important part in vocational guidance practice in this country. Rodger posed two questions about physical makeup. First, has the interviewee any defects of health or physique that may be of occupational importance? Second, how agreeable is his appearance, his bearing and his speech?

Attainments relate to educational achievements and those outside the narrow classroom sense. This information can be obtained from the interviewee. Rodger also includes occupational training and experience for those already at work. General intelligence means general intellectual capacity and Rodger advocates the use of tests to establish this, whilst using the interview to explore how far this intelligence is normally used. Special aptitudes cover mechanical/manual dexterity, facility in the use of words or figures, talent for drawing or music. Tests can be used to measure some of these aptitudes, although Rodger warns against too much occupational significance being attached to these special aptitudes. General intelligence is more important.

To what extent are the client's interests intellectual, practical/ constructional, physically active, social or artistic? Rodger says that interests have to be treated cautiously as they may be short-lived and unsoundly based, and may not relate to actual accomplishments. Indeed, he asks whether drives such as doing good or making money are more relevant but concludes that there is a fivefold classification of occupations:

1 those with intellectual processes, e.g. clerical work
2 those of mainly practical/constructional type, e.g. engineering
3 those of mainly physically active type, e.g. farming
4 those essentially involving some relationship with other people, e.g. sales
5 those of a mainly artistic kind.

Disposition has to do with personality, temperament and character, whilst circumstances refers to situations where the individual has a particular opportunity like a family business.

The theory of work adjustment and person–environment confidence

Lloyd Lofquist originally developed the theory arising from a work adjustment project (at the University of Minnesota in 1959) to study the work adjustment of vocational rehabilitation clients. Since then, in conjunction with Renée Dawis, the theory has been refined to include person–environment correspondence. Dawis (1996) traces the theory's development. It began by emphasising the individual's needs and how these were satisfied by reinforcers, e.g. pay, which are extracted from the environment by use of his/her capabilities. At the heart of the theory of work adjustment (TWA) is the contention that person and environment attempt to achieve and maintain correspondence with each other, which should lead to satisfaction.

Integral to the TWA is a matching model, although the emphasis is on the worker. Here aptitude is crucial, and is measured by ability or aptitude tests. Emphasis is also given to values as an expression of the individual's needs. Values and abilities combine to form personality structure. The environment structure is based on the characteristic abilities and values of the people working in a set place. The TWA is concerned with issues of change within the individual and the workplace leading to discorrespondence, and as such the theory can be seen as a system type process model. It does take into account stages of development. It suggests that the first two decades of life be called differentiation, where capabilities, requirements and style unfold. This is followed by stability, with abilities and values stable but change likely to occur in skills and needs. Finally, decline occurs with physiological changes taking place due to ageing.

Dawis (1996) claims that TWA can be used for career assessment, i.e. matching, and for career counselling. Brown (1996) describes TWA as well constructed and comprehensive although he does add that it is rooted in learning theories which seem too simplistic to much of modern psychology.

Holland's theory

John Holland's work on vocational choice dates back to 1959 and has continued unabated since that time. Osipow (1983) describes his theory as based on career choices representing an extension of personality and holds that there is an attempt to implement personal behavioural styles in the context of work.

Holland's (1973) assumptions underlying his theory are:

1 In our culture, most persons can be categorised as one of six types: realistic, investigative, artistic, social, enterprising or conventional.
2 There are six types of environment: realistic, investigative, artistic, social, enterprising or conventional. As people of the same type congregate, they help create an environment typical of their particular type.
3 People search for environments that will let them exercise their skills and abilities, express their attitudes and values, and take on agreeable problems and roles.
4 A person's behaviour is determined by an interaction between his personality and the characteristics of his environment.

In addition, Holland refers to some other key concepts:

- *Consistency*   Some types have more in common with other types. Figure 2.1 demonstrates the relationship between types. Correlations between the types are indicated.
- *Differentiation*   Some people and some environments are much closer to one type, whilst other people and environments are much more a mixture of types.
- *Congruence*   There are degrees of fit between people and environments, e.g. a realistic type fits best into a realistic environment and next best into an investigative environment.

Holland describes his six personality types in some detail. He says that each is a model orientation based on coping mechanisms, psychological needs and motives, self-concepts, life history, vocational and educational goals, preferred occupational roles, aptitudes and intelligence.

- *Realistic*   Physically strong, unsociable, aggressive, lacks verbal skills but has good motor coordination. Has conventional political and economic values. Examples of occupations: surveyor, car mechanic, plumbing, radio operator.
- *Investigative*   Needs to understand, likes thinking through problems, task oriented, has unconventional values and attitudes. Examples of occupations: geologist, editor of scientific journal, design engineer.
- *Artistic*   Tends to be introverted, rejects conventional values but has high ideals. Avoids problems that are highly structured or require gross physical skills, has a need for individualistic expression. Examples of occupations: author, composer, stage director, commercial artist.
- *Social*   Sociable, responsible, religious, has verbal and interpersonal skills, prefers to solve problems through feelings. Examples of occupations: counsellor, social worker, speech therapist, teacher.
- *Enterprising*   Uses verbal skills for selling, leading, likes ambiguous social tasks, great concern for power and status. Examples of occupations: TV producer, estate agent, buyer, hotel manager.
- *Conventional*   Conforming, likes well-structured tasks, values material possessions and status, prefers structured verbal and numerical activities

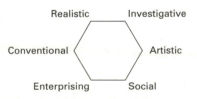

Figure 2.1   *Relationships among types*

and subordinate roles. Examples of occupations: bank clerk, statistician, quality controller.

Holland states that a person's primary direction of choice is determined by the model type he most resembles, e.g. an investigative/social combination might be represented in a science teacher. This determines the choice of role within the environment. Holland also perceives the realistic and investigative types as more stable in their choices, whilst enterprising, social and artistic types have higher aspirations. He also associates high educational aspirations with investigative, social and artistic types as opposed to realistic. Creativity is most associated with investigative and artistic.

Working environments are largely created by the typical characteristics of those working within them. There is a mutual attraction operating which can be seen when employers recruit in their own image and choose the sort of people who will fit in. Likewise, applicants try and sense whether they can relate to fellow workers when deciding whether to accept a job or not. Holland does point out that tasks and situations, and not just people, are important when it comes to choice.

There is more subtlety in Holland's types and environments than may appear at first sight. He perceives individuals in terms of a first, second and third type and also states that work environments are made up of a combination of environmental models. Thus a realistic environment, for instance, may have elements of an investigative environment as well.

Holland emphasises early childhood development. He stated that parents' personality patterns were likely to determine the stability of the individual's personality pattern. Change does take place during people's lives and the types most likely to change are social, enterprising, conventional, artistic, investigative and realistic, in that order.

Holland has always been interested in developing instruments for use in vocational guidance, arising from his research work. The Self Directed Search (1973), the Occupations Finder (1973) and the Vocational Preference Inventory (1973) are the fruit of this interest. Spokane (1996) draws attention to the many studies of Holland's work, which have for the most part been supportive. He maintains that theory is 'unique in employing a comprehensive and integrated assessment system based on empirical research' (1996: 62). Brown (1996) describes Holland's theory as well constructed, although he is critical that Holland does not examine the developmental forces that results in personality types.

Developmental theories

Super

Donald Super is probably the major figure in occupational choice theory. His work is extensive, spread over a long period and based on research on both sides of the Atlantic. His original 10 propositions were amended to 12 (Super and Bachrach, 1957), and subsequently to 14 (Super, 1990), and are still valid in Super's estimation. It is not necessary to list all these propositions in order to understand Super's ideas, although it is worth considering the most significant (Super et al., 1996: 123–6):

Proposition 4   Vocational preferences and competencies, the situations in which people live and work, and hence their self-concepts, change with time and experience (although self-concepts are generally fairly stable from late adolescence until late maturity), making choice and adjustment a continuous process.

Proposition 6   The nature of the career pattern (that is, the occupational level attained and the sequence, frequency and duration of trial and stable jobs), is determined by the individual's parental socio-economic level, mental ability and personality characteristics, and by the opportunities to which he is exposed.

Proposition 7   Success in coping with the demands of the environment and of the organism in the context of any given life-career stage depends on the readiness of the individual to cope with these demands (that is, on his or her career maturity). Career maturity is a constellation of physical, psychological and social characteristics; psychologically, it is both cognitive and affective. It includes the degree of success in coping with the demands of earlier stages and substages of career development and especially with the most recent.

Proposition 9   Development through the life stages can be guided, partly by facilitating the process of maturation of abilities and interests, and partly by aiding in reality testing and in the development of self-concept.

Proposition 10   The process of vocational development is essentially that of developing and implementing a self-concept: it is a compromise process in which the self-concept is a product of the interaction of inherited aptitudes, neural and endocrine makeup, opportunity to play various roles, and evaluations of the extent to which the results of role playing meet with the approval of superiors and fellows.

Proposition 12   Work satisfactions and life satisfactions depend upon the extent to which the individual finds adequate outlets for his abilities, interests, personality traits and values; they depend upon his establishment in a type of work, a work situation, and a way of life in which he can play the kind of role which his growth and exploratory experiences have led him to consider congenial and appropriate.

Proposition 14   Work and occupation provide a focus for personality organisation for most men and women, although for some people this focus is peripheral, incidental or even non-existent and other foci such as social activities and the home are central.

Super's developmental approach is founded on five life stages, and these are described below.

1 *Growth* (birth to 14)   Fantasy (4–10): needs are dominant. Interest (11–12). Capacity (13–14): abilities are considered as well as job requirements.
2 *Exploration* (15–24)   Tentative (15–17): tentative choices are made and tried out in fantasy, discussions and work. Transition (18–21): reality factors are given more attention as the individual enters work, training or further education. Trial (21–24): an apparently suitable choice is tried out.
3 *Establishment* (24–44)   Trial (24–30): job (or jobs) are likely to be tested for suitability. Stabilisation (31–44): a pattern emerges and the individual attempts to secure his position in work.
4 *Maintenance* (44–64)   Work position is consolidated.
5 *Decline* (65+)   Retirement or reduction in work role.

Subsequently, Super (1981) has used the concept of role to illustrate the variety of ways in which the individual conducts his life. In his life-career rainbow (Figure 2.2) there are nine potential roles which can be occupied at some stage. These roles are conducted within four principal theatres: home, community, education and work. This is a very helpful way of conceptualising the different areas of life experience and how they interact. It puts work into perspective by showing that it is one of many roles that we might adopt. Many people have been deprived of this role by unemployment, but this does not leave them without an identity or a role. It also illustrates how roles can conflict and create problems, e.g. work role and parent role.

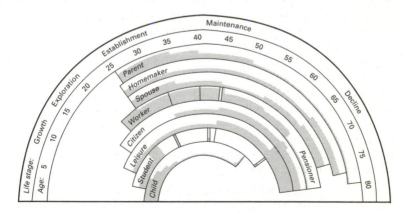

Figure 2.2 *Life-career rainbow (Super): the dark portions of each role indicate the time involved*

By conceptualising life as a series of roles, the rainbow does enable both women and men to see their lives as one of reconciling the demands of family, employment, parents, the community, one's interests, domestic life etc. However, it does not take into account the challenges of mid-life, for example. The life stages assume a smooth progression through establishment to maintenance before decline in later years. This does not accord with much that has happened in recent years with mass redundancy, unemployment, retraining and the growing number of mature students in higher education, whilst increased levels of divorce and single parenthood have also had a great impact on adult life.

More recently, Super (1990) developed another model of career development which he called a segmental model reflecting its mix of different theories. He termed it the archway model (Figure 2.3), emphasising its synthetic nature. The left-hand side represents psychological factors and the right-hand side the societal factors. Super stresses that the two columns interact and that lines should be drawn representing the dynamic interaction of individual and society.

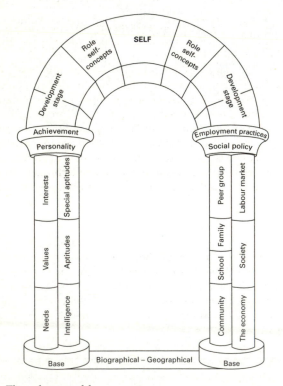

Figure 2.3   *The archway model*

The capitals of the columns represent the integration of each aspect of the individual and of society, whilst the arch is the career. The development stage on the left is childhood and adolescence and that on the right is young adulthood and maturity. During these stages, the self-concept is developing and forms the keystone of the arch, the self. It is interesting to note that Super describes the cement for the arch as learning theory and in particular social learning theory (Mitchell et al., 1979). Thus interactive experiential learning, self-concept and occupations concept formation take place through the interaction of the individual and the environment.

Osipow (1983) regards Super's theory as a well-ordered, highly systematic representation of the processes of vocational motivation, although he felt that he had given insufficient attention to social and economic factors that influence career decisions. Since then, Super (1981) has produced a model that does give weight to situational determinants, i.e. social structure and economic conditions, as well as personal determinants, i.e. interests, values, etc.

Super's work, as we saw earlier, has stimulated the practice of careers programmes. By stressing the developmental nature of occupational choice and the possibility of positive interventions in this process, Super has laid a theoretical basis for careers education.

Salomone (1996) reviews Super's theory and describes it as elusive, because of the changes Super made over time. Most of his original propositions were retained, but three were dropped and others were added later. Super's life stages are open to criticism, mainly based on evidence of mid-life career changes which differ from his description of the maintenance stage. Salomone is also critical of Super's later definition of career which 'has limited usefulness' because it was so broad and all-inclusive. Acknowledgement is made of Super's major contribution to vocational psychology, whilst also recognising that there are inconsistencies in his work. Brown (1996) is also mixed in his assessment of Super's contribution which he describes as the segmental legacy of a thinker who is brilliant but whose theory is not well constructed and whose constructs are not carefully defined.

Gottfredson

A more recent developmental theory has been formulated by Lynda Gottfredson (1981; 1996). She describes her theory as 'Circumscription and compromise: a developmental theory of occupational aspirations'. Figure 2.4 demonstrates the relationship between the theoretical constructs she uses and represents a summary of her developmental theory. The constructs are as follows:

1 *Self-concept* This includes both present and future perceptions of self. Our self-concept is not always fully articulated as it represents the totality of different ways of seeing ourselves.

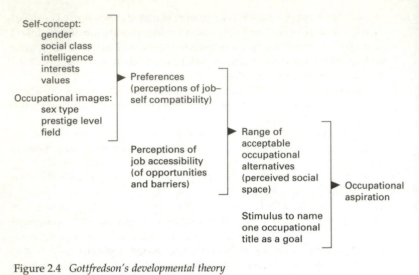

Figure 2.4 *Gottfredson's developmental theory*

2 *Occupational images or stereotypes* Based on generalisations we have about jobs. These images are linked together to give a cognitive map of occupations, based on a few simple dimensions.
3 *Occupational preferences* We assess the compatibility of occupations with the images of who we would like to be and how much effort we are willing to exert to enter those occupations.
4 *Perceived accessibility of occupations* Refers to the chances we see of entering occupations and thus realism.
5 *Occupational alternatives* The product of job compatibility and accessibility, and can be seen to be in social space, i.e. the sort of person we would like to be or are willing to be in the eyes of family, peers and wider society.

Gottfredson maintains that most people seem to share a cognitive map of occupations, based upon research conducted by Holland (1973), along dimensions of prestige and sex type (this map, of course, applies to American society and may not be true for other cultures).

The formation of self-concept and occupational preferences begins early in life, and represents a general developmental process, but with some difference in rates depending on intelligence. Gottfredson applies five principles to this development:

• *Concreteness/abstractness progression* Children progress from intuitive thinking to more abstract thinking. Thus, vocational development can be seen as growth in the capacity to apprehend and organise relevant information about self and jobs.

- *Interactive development of self-concept and vocational preferences*   The development of self-concept and vocational preferences are intimately linked.
- *Overlapping differentiation–incorporation sequences*   Each new stage gives people the opportunity to incorporate more abstract concepts of self arising from the previous stage.
- *Irreversible progressive circumscription (elimination) of alternatives*   To a large extent, vocational choice is the elimination of alternatives from further consideration.
- *Ability to display but not to verbalise spontaneously the bases of preference*   People have difficulty verbalising why they rate occupations as better or worse.

Gottfredson's life stages are as follows:

1 *Orientation to size and power* (3–5)   Children begin to associate power with adulthood rather than magic and with occupational roles, i.e. becoming a big person. This is usually linked to the same-sex parent.
2 *Orientation to sex roles* (6–8)   At this stage, children begin to grasp the concept of sex roles and stereotypes emerge. Children's occupational preferences reflect a concern with doing what is appropriate for one's sex. This is likely to be linked with a consolidation of a sense of identity.
3 *Orientation to social valuation* (9–13)   Youngsters are very sensitive to peer group evaluations. They begin to recognise prestige differences among jobs as well as social class and ability differences among people. There is a growing concern with the level of occupation and this is intimately connected with social class, and in most cases youngsters will take the group of which they are a member as their reference group. Gottfredson concludes that youngest children's preferences are indeed very childish but they are already sex typed. Older children's preferences may be unstable as far as particular occupational titles are concerned, but they reject preferences for level of work.
4 *Orientation to the internal unique self* (14+)   By adolescence, a zone of acceptable occupational alternatives has been established. The next stage of development is to carve out a personal identity and to arrive at more specific occupational choices. This involves more independence from external influences such as parents. It is a period of instability and uncertainty, and one of greater complexity and integration.

Compromise is an issue because the jobs people want may sometimes be very different from the jobs available to them. Gottfredson maintains that people focus their attention on occupations in their social space, until these have been exhausted. She also states that information gathering about jobs tends to be confined to the time when decisions have to be made. Finally, she says that readily available sources of information are surveyed first, i.e. parents.

The compromise process is made easier by most people's realistic view of the labour market. Gottfredson suggests three principles operating:

1 Some aspects of self-concept are more central than others and will take priority when compromising occupational goals. Gender is the most strongly protected aspect of self, if delivered by the maintenance of one's social standing or worth; that is, one's social class and ability self-concepts. One's identity, as portrayed through one's personality and specific interests and abilities on the job, is the most flexible.
2 Exploration of job options ends with the implementation of a satisfactory choice, not necessarily the optimal potential choice. So we have a range of occupations potentially acceptable.
3 People accommodate psychologically to the compromises they make. It means that by their late twenties, the workforce seem relatively content.

As regards practice, Gottfredson advocates:

1 The use of interest inventories, ability tests and other experiences to help youngsters discover and verify their interests, ability and personality traits when unsure of themselves.
2 Take into account the cognitive development of clients when assessing the best procedure to follow.
3 Many cases of indecision can be attributed to a number of reasons, i.e. aspirations incompatible to interests and abilities; women who have not questioned traditional ways of combining family and work; middle/ upper-class youngsters having to aspire to jobs beyond their ability etc.
4 Greater help with how to get occupational information and how to be interviewed.
5 Finally, because by age 13 most youngsters circumscribe their aspirations by sex type and prestige, she asks where that leaves the careers counsellor. Should one accept the status quo or attempt to reshape aspirations?

Gottfredson (1996) suggests that her theory highlights the need for career counsellors to encourage both exploration and realism, and she emphasises the importance of information. Gottfredson describes a tension for careers counsellors, who on the one hand may be committed to helping their clients move away from the earlier circumscription of their lives, and yet on the other hand need to accept the reality of necessary compromise.

Learning theories

Social learning theory of career decision making

In the late 1970s, social learning theory was applied to occupational choice by a group of American researchers. Their work was published by Mitchell et al. (1979) and they claim that their theory tries to encompass a complete process and not some phase of it. The theory is said to explain the development of career aspirations and clarifies the role of decision making. It also takes into account economic and sociological variables as well as personality theory. This approach grew out of the work of behavioural psychology; thus it is claimed that people learn not just from the consequences of their own responses but also from the observation of other people's behaviour and its consequences for them. Mitchell et al. (1979) state that four factors influence career decision making:

1   genetic endowment, i.e. race, sex, intelligence and special abilities
2   environmental conditions and events, e.g. family experience and training opportunities
3   learning experiences, e.g. instrumental and associative learning
4   task approach skills, e.g. learning skills.

Three types of consequences arise from these four influences:

• self-observation generalisations, e.g. I'm good at English
• task approach skills, e.g. seeking information about work
• actions, e.g. applying for a course of study.

Genetic endowment and environmental conditions are clearly beyond the control of the client or counsellor, but this is not the case with learning experiences and task approach skills. Instrumental learning experiences are those where the individual acts on the environment so as to produce certain outcomes. On the other hand, associative learning experiences occur when the individual pairs two events so that he or she associates a previously neutral situation with some positive or negative reaction. Task approach skills cover a wide range, for instance thought processes and performance standards. Clearly, there are many ways of improving these skills through individual or group means.

Self-observation generalisations result from learning experiences and, of course, are not always accurate. Values are a type of self-observation generalisation. Using interests and profiling them by means of questionnaires is a usual and valid way of establishing a pattern of these generalisations.

Social learning theory has a number of implications for counsellors:

1   Occupational placement is the result of a complex interaction of genetic components, environmental events and conditions and learning experiences which result in the development of various task approach skills.
2   Career selection is a mutual process influenced not only by decisions made by each individual involved but also by social forces which affect occupational availability and requirements. People select, and are selected by, occupations.

3 Career selection is a lifelong process. It does not take place at one point in time, but is shaped by events and decisions that occur from infancy through to the retirement years. As with Super, the development aspects are stressed from the early years to later adulthood.

4 Career selection is caused, not accidental, but the interaction of causal events is so complex that the prediction of occupational selection for any one individual is virtually impossible with any degree of certainty. If Krumboltz is correct, this makes traditional vocational guidance, which was largely based on prediction and forecast, an invalid exercise.

5 Career indecision is due to the unsatisfactory nature or insufficient number of career learning experiences, or to the fact that the person has not yet learned and applied a systematic way of making career decisions. Indecision is a natural result of not having had certain learning experiences. An undecided person has no reason to feel guilty or inadequate. The ability to make career decisions is directly related to relevant learning experiences. The implication from this is clear: that the school or counsellor can help provide some of these experiences through offering work experience.

6 Career counselling is not merely a process of matching personal characteristics with existing job characteristics, but instead is a process of opening up new learning experiences and motivating a client to initiate career-relevant exploratory activities. This statement expands the role of vocational guidance from diagnosis and assessment to a broader developmental role.

7 The responsibilities of a career counsellor, then, are as follows: to help the client learn a rational sequence of career decision-making skills; to help the client arrange an appropriate sequence of career-relevant exploratory learning experiences; and to teach the client how to evaluate the personal consequences of these learning experiences.

Mitchell and Krumboltz (1996) redefined the theory as learning theory of career choice and counselling in order to provide a guide for practice. They proposed that:

1 People need to expand their capabilities and interests, not make decisions on existing characteristics only.

2 People need to prepare for changing work tasks, not assume that occupations will remain stable.

3 People need to be empowered to take action, not merely to be given a diagnosis.

4 Career counsellors need to play a major role in dealing with all career problems, not just occupational selection. As such, they should promote client learning.

Career learning theory

Law (1996a) has produced a new theory which he claims is appropriate to the present day. Like Super, he sets out a number of propositions:

1 Some career development activities depend upon relatively basic capacities, in the sense that these capacities are innate, or are easier to acquire, or can be acquired without the benefit of much prior learning.
2 Other activities depend on more developed capacities, in the sense that they are needed to deal with more complex, dynamic, abstract or emotionally laden experiences.
3 Whether basic or developed, these capacities include both intellectual and behavioural elements, but they also include capacities to acknowledge and manage one's own and others' feelings.
4 The more basic activities require that a person is able to sense career-related information and impressions, and to sift that material into recognisable patterns that can become the basis for action.
5 The more developed activities require a person to focus the material more tightly (for example, by differentiating elements in terms of point of view or ascribed value) and to understand it (for example, by being able to identify causes and probable effects in specific scenarios).
6 Some career development activities require no more than the basic capacities: such activities can be characterised as a 'sense, sift and act' process used by everyone in more or less routine situations.
7 But everyone will, from time to time, need to engage more developed capacities, where the action is critical or its ramifications are extensive. Here sensing and sifting need to be extended into a 'focus, understand and act' process.
8 The more developed capacities cannot be engaged unless some basic capacities have been successfully developed to support them. In simple terms, a person cannot concentrate upon and properly grasp information she or he has not first sensed and sifted. In more complex terms, the capacity to focus and understand requires a foundation of prior learning.
9 Where prior learning has not been accomplished, or has been accomplished in a form which distorts rather than represents the information, further development may be hindered. Put specifically: a person is likely to misunderstand on the basis of flimsy or misperceived evidence. Put generally: the sifting of knowledge into stereotyped or other habitually biased frames will distort further development.
10 Like other learning, career development can be educated. A programme which builds a cycle or cycles of learning, developing from sensing through sifting and focusing to understanding, will equip a person with an educated repertoire of capacities to support career development actions.

The developing repertoire of career development capacities is set out in Figure 2.5.

Understanding	8 Anticipating consequences
	7 Developing explanations
Focusing	6 Taking one's own view
	5 Dealing with points of view
Sifting	4 Using concepts
	3 Making comparisons
Sensing	2 Assembling sequences
	1 Gathering information

Figure 2.5 *Repertoire of career development capacities*

Sensing is based on the assumption that we work from information about work, role and self. Gathering information begins early in life and forms maps which guide us in later life. With assembling sequences, narrative becomes important, i.e. career is then a narratable story, moving across a mappable terrain from episode to episode, each with its own decisions and transitions.

Sifting includes making comparisons which form constructs, for example stereotypes. Constructs move career thinking towards the issue of causality. Using career-related concepts raises a series of questions about where one might work, what one might do, how one might do it etc.

Focusing recognises that career learning cannot occur in a social vacuum: it involves dealing with points of view. It requires the individual to be exposed to facts and opinion about work and role. This then is related to self by means of taking one's own view. Law asks why a view is formed and answers that it must be salient, i.e. in tune, valued and credible (it makes sense).

Understanding is necessary in order to proceed to sensible action. This requires developing explanations by asking 'Why do I want to do job A?' etc., which constitutes personal narrative, rather than by observing 'To succeed in job A, people need to be highly numerate' etc., which constitutes meta-narrative. Finally, career learning requires a progression from attempting explanation of the past to anticipating future consequences.

Law describes a number of practical implications of his theory:

1 Foundation learning should begin in the primary school, with an emphasis on sensing and sifting.
2 Connecting learning: there are many openings within the curriculum to provide opportunities for mapping narrative etc.
3 Pivotal learning: which requires systematically revisiting all levels of sensing, sifting, focusing and understanding, in increasing detail and depth.
4 Recovery learning: rebuilding because of lost opportunities.

Law concludes that if we do not help people with their career learning earlier, we should not be surprised if, later, help needs more time than we can readily give.

It is very interesting to see that Law (1999) revisits the DOTS analysis (see Chapter 6) in the light of the development of career learning theory. Post-DOTS thinking also needs to take into account contemporary policy concerns that Law identifies. These include changing global conditions, flexible career management, social exclusion and lifelong learning. New theories such as career learning theory and community interaction theory have implications for the curriculum and 'suggest the reassembly of DOTS coverage into a manageable but valid learning process which can sustain action' (Law 1999).

Opportunity structure theory

Ken Roberts (1977; 1997) has made a notable contribution to a sociological understanding of career development. He has focused attention away from the individual choice towards the social structures significant to the individual's entry to employment. Hence, he describes his theory in terms of opportunity structure. The theory is based on the following assertions:

1 Neither school leavers nor adults typically choose their jobs in any meaningful sense; they simply take what is available. Job preferences are not mere matters of individual taste but are determined by a system of stratification.
2 The occupational opportunities open to any school leaver are structured by a number of factors, the most important of which is that the individual's educational attainments and his/her freedom of occupational choice are really strictly limited.
3 School leavers stand in varying degrees of social proximity to different types of occupations. These varying degrees of social proximity have nothing to do with the ambitions of the individuals concerned. They are inherent in the structure of the educational institutions that the young people are leaving and the occupational institutions they are entering.

Thus, Roberts maintains that for all individuals, whatever their qualifications, the social structure determines their eventual occupation. He points to socialisation creating a climate of expectation which is associated with particular educational careers and internalised by each individual. Their aspirations are the result of anticipatory socialisation which takes place first in the family, with most children learning traditional sex roles and values related to work.

Roberts is, in fact, following the sociological tradition of conceptualising occupational entry in terms of selection, allocation and placement. However, he does pose some crucial questions concerning the belief that

individuals choose their occupations and the apparent acquiescence of so
many individuals who enter poorly paid and boring jobs (or have no jobs
at all). Inevitably, the answer lies in the process of socialisation which
adjusts the expectations and aspirations of individuals by means of gender
roles, ethnic stereotyping and social class images within the family, the
education system and the media.

Roberts's work is of particular interest because he discusses the role of
the Careers Service at some length. For instance, he says that, irrespective
of their sincerity, careers workers cannot simply help young people towards
self-understanding and jobs in which they will optimise their own values.
Career workers either direct young people towards jobs they are structurally obliged to enter, in which case they are objectively acting as part of
the social control apparatus, or encourage young people to develop aims
that discord with opportunities they eventually encounter. In the latter
event, this radical cultural work may one day help to precipitate structural
change. Alternatively, it might simply leave young people maladjusted
to the occupations they are pragmatically obliged to enter. Careers work
cannot be neutral.

There is an element of determinism in Roberts's work on occupational
choice that can be disconcerting to those working in vocational guidance.
He seems to be saying that the structural constraints are such that
individuals have no real choice, and hence vocational guidance is largely
an illusion. Certainly, he advocates careers officers moving away from a
developmental role based on careers education and adopting the role of
placement officer (Roberts, 1977). This has been strongly contested by Daws
(1977), with some success.

Daws (1977) does provide a powerful critique of Roberts's opportunity
structure theory. First, he questions whether it can be described as a theory,
as Roberts himself has suggested that it will not fit all situations, thus
weakening its comprehensiveness. Second, Daws maintains that Roberts
does not take into account the rapidity of contemporary social and economic
change, and with it the degree of social mobility. Third, Daws feels that
Roberts denies the value of psychological theories of occupational choice
without sufficient evidence. Daws sees a place for both disciplines in
providing a comprehensive explanation of occupational choice.

Roberts makes an eloquent and persuasive case for his opportunity
structure perspective. However, if his own empirical evidence is examined,
this is found to be lacking. His original study (1968) was based on a survey
of 196 men aged 14 to 23 in a London borough in 1965. There is information
lacking on this sample – for instance, ethnic background, educational
qualifications, social class. It is also notable that women were not included.
In order to present a theory as positively as Roberts does, a much sounder
empirical base is required.

Since his controversial article in 1977, Roberts has written extensively on
issues to do with young people and work. His most recent article is worth
examining in detail (Roberts, 1997). The title, 'Prolonged transitions to

uncertain destinations', sums up the themes he considers. Prolonged transitions have largely been the result of the appetite of young people and their parents for qualifications, something that is true of virtually all social backgrounds. This appetite has been influenced by the demands of a changing occupational structure.

With prolonged transitions, young people's biographies have been individualised, largely as a result of greater geographical mobility and less predictability of employment opportunities. However, life chances remain as dependent as ever on social class backgrounds and attainments in compulsory education, in Roberts's words. Finally, Roberts highlights how uncertain young people's career prospects have become, and how there is more risk involved. However, this situation has become normal, and Roberts maintains that young people accept this, and indeed welcome the scope this can offer. Careers guidance needs to respond with customised assistance, which can be delivered via a combination of computerised systems and personalised help. Young people can be encouraged to consider all the alternative futures to which they might proceed, rather than be required to make a choice earlier in their lives.

Problems that he identifies are:

1 Jobs deficit, which is likely to remain a general feature of our economy.
2 Pressure on families, with young people being financially dependent on their parents for longer periods owing to delayed entry into paid employment. With increasing numbers of single parents and reconstituted families, this can lead to severe problems.
3 Dead ends, whereby low achievers find it difficult to get anything that offers a real future.

The winners Roberts identifies are girls, who seem better able than boys to cope with the new transition processes; some ethnic minorities of Asian origin; and the children of parents who are both working full-time in good jobs. Roberts identifies this last group as skilled consumers most likely to seek careers advice for their children.

In the last 20 years there has been a great change in the opportunity structure, and Roberts has recognised this and adjusted his interpretation of the occupational choice process accordingly. How far he has moved from his original deterministic position and from his perception of the role of careers guidance is an interesting question.

Community interaction theory

In 1981, Bill Law published an article setting out 'a mid-range focus for theories of career development in young adults'. This was an attempt to bridge differences in thinking between talent matching, humanistic and structural theories of occupational choice which had dominated thinking and practice in the previous 50 years. He rightly pointed to the need for theory to adapt to changes in society and he subsequently explored such trends in a later article (Law, 1984).

Law attempts to bring together what has seemed to be the irreconcilable differences between theories that focus on the individual and those that focus on structural factors. He maintains that the way in which 'who does what' in society is decided is the product of a plurality of interpersonal transactions conducted in local settings and on the basis of interaction within and between groups of which the individual is a member – the community. He accepts that the term 'community' is problematic but stresses that this is the scale at which we conduct our lives. His case is supported by reference to a number of sociological studies of peer groups, schools and communities.

Community acts as a transmitter of motivation and as a modifier of social functioning. In the first instance, Law states that a great deal of the process of identifying motivation for career development occurs in mid-range transactions involving the participation of parents, family, neighbourhood, peer groups and ethnic groups – the ragtag of community. As regards social functioning, he maintains that a particular community can modify the impact of structural factors such as social class and ethnic origin.

Law goes on to state that the community influences individuals in five specific ways:

1 expectations via the family or peer group by means of cues, pressures or enhancements
2 feedback concerning their suitability for different sorts of social roles by means of the images they receive of themselves by being members of certain groups
3 support, reinforcements and encouragements that group membership can entail
4 modelling, the opportunity to meet and understand ways of life outside those of the person's origins, the chance to identify with particular role models
5 information, communication of impressions, images and data which arises from being a member of a particular community, some of which is relevant to employment and training.

Law asserts that his theory adopts a phenomenological perspective in examining careers education. This position suggests that it is necessary to examine individuals' biographies by constructing an ever changing set of representations of self and situation. These constructions are built from the process of interaction with members of the social groups to which the individual belongs. There is, accordingly, no absolutely agreed self or society to arbitrate upon career development. There is only what each individual continuously negotiates from the process of interaction.

Law is arguing for a much less static and fixed state of affairs than previous theorists have maintained. This approach maintains that in order to predict and explain what is important in people's lives, we have to look at their day-to-day encounters with other people. It posits that we are forever changing, in some sense, and that being a member of one particular group, e.g. peer or ethnic group, does not in itself predict aspirations or occupation.

The logical consequence of Law's theory is pluralistic guidance in what he terms an unpredictable society. First, he sees coordination of resources as being of central importance. This means bringing community resources to bear upon the guidance objectives of students and to fill major gaps in the student's experience. Second, the guidance specialist should be an innovator, which means intervening more directly in the system of which they are a part. Finally, Law stresses the need for counselling – in other words, the one-to-one relationship.

In conclusion, the emphasis of this theory is upon networking an awareness of the need to draw upon a multiplicity of sources, and an acceptance that the guidance specialist does not have all the resources or all the answers to meet the client's needs.

Law's bridging theory has a number of attractive features. It seems to relate to people's experiences and includes a wide range of influences. It has practical implications and appears to respond to the complexities and realities of life today. Criticisms could be made that it fails to recognise other groups that are important in some people's lives, e.g. women's groups and the gay community.

A socio-psychological model of career choice and work behaviour

Helen Astin (1984) has produced a model examining the particular experience of women and work. The model has the following characteristics:

1 It attends to both psychological variables (personal characteristics) and the contextual sociological variables (social forces).
2 It draws upon earlier theories.
3 It uses the construct Structure of opportunity as a way of depicting how social forces shape and reshape occupational decisions.
4 It proposes that the occupational behaviour of both genders can be considered in the same way.
5 Finally, it can explain generational changes in the behaviour of groups such as women.

Astin begins by considering the salience of work and quotes Freud in saying that the healthy adult is the one who has the ability to love and to work. She states that it is possible to conceptualise a common set of work motivations for women and men. This supplies the first of four basic constructs to the model (Figure 2.6). The model is developmental, explaining changes in career choice. Two of the constructs are psychological (work motivation and expectations) and the other two are cultural/environmental (sex-role socialisation and the structure of opportunity).

The model is based on four principles:

1 Work behaviour is motivated activity intended to satisfy three basic needs: survival, pleasure and contribution.
2 Career choices are based on expectations concerning the accessibility of alternative forms of work and their relative capacity to satisfy the three basic needs.
3 Expectations are shaped in part by early socialisation through family, childhood play, school experiences and early work experiences, and in part by the perceived structure of opportunity.
4 Expectations developed through socialisation and through early perceptions of the structure of opportunity can be modified by changes in the structure of opportunity, and this modification in expectations can lead to changes in career choice and in work behaviour.

Expectations are important in occupational choice because men and women differ in their work expectations: that is, in their perceptions of what types of work are available or accessible to them and of what types of work can best satisfy their needs.

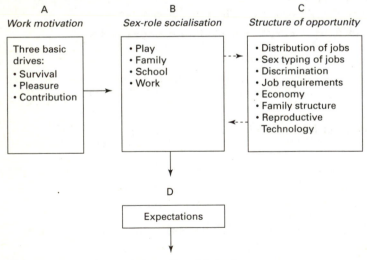

Figure 2.6 *Need-based socio-psychological model of career choice and work behaviour*

Socialisation occurs in play, within the family, at school and at work, and it is here that we see the different experiences of boys and girls. Play, household chores and early paid employment have traditionally been defined and distributed along gender lines. Astin concludes that in the competitive games that boys play is the notion of winning, which translates into the notion of acquiring resources (power, prestige, income) through gainful employment. In contrast, girls' play involves nurturing and caring for others rather than competing with them. Girls learn to satisfy both their pleasure needs and their contribution needs by direct service to others.

The structure of opportunity in the world of work changes and this accounts for the drastic changes in careers that we can observe. It is important to observe the interaction that takes place between this structure and socialisation. The socialisation process probably sets limits to changes in the structure of opportunity, whereas the structure of opportunity influences the values that are transmitted through the socialisation process. This could account for the changes that have taken place in the occupational choices of many women in the last decade.

Astin draws attention to the notion that early socialisation practices have not changed as dramatically as the occupational behaviour of women. Here we must examine changes in the structure of opportunity. The trends she identifies are:

- increased longevity
- declining birthrate
- increasing divorce rate
- proliferation of non-traditional lifestyles
- medical advances and reproductive technology
- codification of women's rights
- changes in the nation's economy.

In summary, Astin returns to needs. She states that the rising divorce rate, the proliferation of non-traditional lifestyles, and changes in the nation's economy, have all had an impact on work behaviour aimed at satisfying the need for survival. As regards pleasure needs, women, because of increased longevity and reduced time spent on child bearing and rearing, now look to paid employment increasingly to satisfy these needs. Looking at contribution needs, Astin states that because our society has tended to undervalue the kinds of occupations traditionally chosen by women, it is not surprising that, as lifestyles have become more diversified and as women's rights have been codified, more women are choosing non-traditional careers that are more highly valued and recognised.

A contextual explanation of career

In recent years careers theory has moved in a new direction (Collin and Young, 1986; 1988) based on the assertion that 'mainstream career theory has taken a limited view of the environment of careers' (Collin, 1997). Collin maintains that traditional career theory, with a few exceptions, has conceptualised the environment too narrowly and not taken into account broader elements such as globalisation and the information technology revolution. Crucially, these mainsteam theories have interpreted the environment as being outside and separate from the individual and the individual is assumed to be a natural entity to be studied detached from its background – in other words, decontextualised.

Collin draws on the 'contextualist world hypothesis' and the work of Pepper (1942). She emphasises the dynamic nature of events and the fact that they are not finished or complete but in process. For this reason,

> discrete units within it cannot be isolated for examination, but the multiplicity of possible connections and interrelationships between events must be recognised. This makes interpretation open-ended, fluid and tentative. Attention must, therefore, be given to the process of meaning making: the continuous generation of new meanings. It also makes the relationship between objectivity and subjectivity problematic. Observer and observed co-exist within the same context or web and hence affect both one another and the wider web. Moreover, their individual perspectives influence what they perceive and how they interpret it: they can identify relationships but not cause and effect. (1997: 439)

Collin uses the metaphors of library and Internet to show the difference between orthodox and contextualist thinking. Thus the library, which is structured by experts and is static and linear, represents the orthodox scientific approach; whilst the Internet, which is an open-ended network, constantly changing, non-linear and organic, represents the contextualist approach.

In explaining career, contextualist theory lays great emphasis on the concept of action (Young et al., 1996). In particular, the notion of joint action can be related to the careers-counsellor/client relationship. Joint action moves beyond the mere interaction to consider how, through language, career identity, values, interests and behaviours are shaped. Collin (1997) talks of a joint construction of meaning with traditional distinctions between subjectivity and objectivity disappearing. With a range of meaning being available, interpretation becomes central to the construction of career. In order to interpret a meaning, it is necessary to know the individual's story: thus a narrative needs to be developed. Young et al. (1996) identify narrative as creating coherence and continuity out of separate actions. They also suggest that the role of emotion in career theories has been undervalued. Emotion energises, regulates and controls actions and provides the key to narratives of career.

There are significant implications arising from contextualism, because it suggests that researchers, theorists, practitioners and clients jointly construct meaning. As such, the client cannot be assumed to be a passive recipient with the professional as the detached 'orchestrator'. Contextualism draws attention to the 'usually asymmetrical power in these relationships, which is often not recognised or addressed in traditional approaches' (1997: 443).

Narrative, dream and myth

Contextualism lays emphasis on the importance of narrative as a way of accessing meaning for the client (Young et al., 1996). It is possible to understand individual narratives as part of a wider socio-psychological perspective. Gothard (1999) draws attention to the work of Campbell (1998), Levinson et al. (1978) and May (1993) who have demonstrated the important role that myth still plays in our lives and linked this to the notion of the dream. The dream constitutes a personal myth, an imagined drama with the individual as the central character in a complex world. Inevitably, the early youthful dream becomes challenged by reality and in mid-life it needs to be re-examined and conformed – a task that may be painful. Career counselling can play a role at this life stage (Gothard, 1996), but there are significant factors that a counsellor needs to bear in mind when working with such clients. Levinson et al. (1978) showed that Jung's work on individuation helps understand the often deep-seated crisis that may be occurring within the client.

Cochran (1997) advocates a narrative approach to career counselling and this is supported by Savickas (1993) in discussing careers work in the postmodern era. Helping the client to identify themes in their life, with the overarching theme being the search for identity, arises from the approach. By identifying the client's dream, the counsellor is tapping into the meta-narrative of myths which locate us in the present and future. It is more appropriate to work with older clients in this way.

Gothard (1996; 1999) draws on psychodynamic concepts in exploring career development. This follows the work of Watkins and Savickas (1990) who have argued the case for psychodynamic career counselling. However, they are critical of the failure of this type of theory to significantly influence research and practice in careers guidance.

Conclusion: career development theory and practice

As Watts et al. (1981) point out, practitioners in most fields tend to be impatient with theory and to resent attempts to intrude theoretical considerations into their work. Yet, as we have seen, theory has helped to mould the way in which careers advisers have worked. In one sense, it does not appear to help the practitioner that there are so many different theories, especially when they can present very different explanations for occupational choice. However, in another sense, this variety of theories does reflect the complexity of the process that is being examined. It also illustrates the fact that we can only understand occupational choice, in a dynamic context, in terms of change – economic, political, social and psychological.

Law (1984) illustrates the need to see careers theory and practice within a wider context by linking what careers advisers do to the theoretical assumptions used to justify doing it, to changes in society surrounding the introduction of that approach, and finally to the values or ideologies relating to each approach. He postulates that there have been four different modes of helping with regard to careers education and counselling. These four models have grown out of the prevailing ideology and the nature of that particular society. Each mode has been underpinned by a particular theory of occupational choice which has led to a particular form of practice. The original mode of helping was via matching techniques, underpinned by differential theories which were responding to a scientific, rationalist ideology operating within a technological and expanding economy. In Britain, this applied to the first 60 years of the twentieth century.

The second mode arose from societies becoming more problematic and therefore more questioning. Thus, in the 1960s, we see humanistic ideologies becoming more dominant, with an emphasis on open exploration and a respect for the individual's freedom to choose. Law describes the dominant theories as being phenomenological and holistic, with Super and Carl Rogers being especially influential. A move from matching techniques to a client-centred approach took place, linked to a greater emphasis on experiential learning.

The mid 1970s saw the beginnings of the first large-scale unemployment since the war, and with it a move towards a functionalist ideology and a recognition of the restricted nature of many people's lives. Sociology led the way with regard to providing an appropriate theory, one which stemmed from the notion of a prescriptive social structure which labelled individuals with little account of their actual worth.

The mode of helping suggested by Law as appropriate to the 1980s is based upon using the community as a resource on which to build up a series of networks in order to assist individuals in choosing an appropriate occupation. He sees the prevailing ideology as pluralist, based on a recognition that society is very diverse and that there are many groups, institutions and individuals who can contribute to job choosing and finding. Rapid social change leads to unpredictable societies: for instance, parents find it difficult to help their children because their experience is so different a generation later.

Subsequently, Law (1996a) has suggested the need for a career learning theory to complement the earlier groups of career development theories. He acknowledges the growth of an increasingly problematic career structure and states that this new theory adds to the terms in which thinking may be framed. Gothard and Mignot (1999) have linked career learning theory to the FIRST framework, a model of guidance introduced by Bedford (1982). This demonstrates the congruence between the theory of career development and a model of guidance, making it possible for practitioners to relate theory more easily to practice. Putting career learning theory into a wider context, Law (1999) demonstrates the increasing trend for career work to be based in a curriculum setting, whilst maintaining its traditional place in a guidance setting. The development of career management modules by university careers services is an example of this trend.

There are many theories relevant to careers guidance; they have developed over time in response to changing contexts and can be seen as having varying relevance to today's clients. What is certain is that no single theory is adequate to explain fully the complex processes of occupational choice and career development that take place in our rapidly changing world. The search continues!

3

WORKING WITH INDIVIDUALS

Setting the context

This chapter begins by exploring the wider context for working with individuals who seek help with 'career'. The chapter moves on to identify the frameworks for career helping that are most commonly used by UK-based practitioners. Consideration is then given to how we define career helping, together with the competing 'world views' that inform our definitions. Specific career helping strategies are described, and the chapter concludes by discussing the role and function of supervision for career helpers. Throughout this chapter the generic term 'career helping' is used as an alternative to more common descriptors such as 'careers guidance'. The reasons for this will become evident in what follows.

The socio-economic context of career helping

As Chapter 1 has indicated, our notion of what constitutes 'career' is changing. Theorists influenced by postmodernism (Payne and Edwards, 1996; Savickas, 1993) and constructivism (Chen, 1997; Collin, 1996; Peavy, 1993) are increasingly defining 'career' in provisional and localised terms. The notions of 'the subjective career' and 'the fragmented career' have become popular precisely because they serve to reflect the uncertainties that many individuals experience in the post-bureaucratic age (Arnold and Jackson, 1997). As part of this new thinking there is evidence of a growing concern with theories of 'self' (Chen, 1997; Edwards and Payne, 1997; Meijers, 1997). This is not surprising because if 'career' is fragmenting then this presents a fundamental challenge to traditional conceptions of 'self' that assume stability and continuity of career choice and development. On this basis, working with individuals and their 'career' is highly problematic: if 'career' is no longer stable and tangible, then the rationale for helping and assisting individuals becomes uncertain.

Furthermore, there are many ways of working with individuals in the context of 'career' and there are many expectations held by individuals seeking 'career' help. A simple classification includes the following activities: careers counselling; careers guidance; careers advice; careers information. However, there is evidence to suggest that these activities remain ill-defined and often undifferentiated in the minds of both clients and practitioners (Bates, 1998; DfEE, 1998a). For example, if I seek careers guidance, do I expect to receive specific advice and information? Does my career helper have the same set of expectations? Indeed, what sort of help would I expect other than advice and information about 'career'? There is an immediate irony here. Although many clients seeking help with 'career' expect advice and information, in retrospect they often express a sense of regret and frustration: 'If only my careers *adviser* had *counselled* me!'; 'I didn't really know what I wanted to do at the time!' Stories such as these, apocryphal or otherwise, continue to beset career helping. These stories also relate to other stories associated with 'career': Yosser Hughes's mantra 'giz a job' in the television series 'Boys from the Blackstuff' has become part of everyday discourse; Billy's interview with his youth employment officer in the film *Kes* presents a powerful, albeit negative metaphor for 'career helping'. Indeed, Yosser's and Billy's stories exemplify Roberts's (1977; 1997) view that 'career' is a middle-class construct and that career helping can be divided into two broad categories: job advice and careers guidance, the former being the necessary pragmatic response to the needs of those who find themselves in the secondary labour market.

The foregoing demonstrates that the expectations of all parties involved in the career helping process are myriad. Thus, not only is 'career' problematic in terms of its fragmentation as a socio-economic activity, it is also problematic in terms of how it is defined and perceived by individuals as a context for helping.

The socio-political context of career helping

Career helping is not an isolated activity. It relates to and is influenced by socio-political developments and trends. Indeed, as Chapter 6 demonstrates, career helping has increasingly been incorporated within government economic and educational policy initiatives (see also Harris, 1999; Stacey and Mignot, 2000). According to Watts (1996b), career helping is inevitably political as it is implicated in the dual processes of social control and social change. For example, in the statutory sector (i.e. the Careers Service) the career helping interaction has progressively been targeted at specific age groups and backgrounds of client. As a result the required outcomes of the career helping interaction have become more specific over the past decade. Thus, there is a 'managerial' dimension to the career helping process which, according to Payne and Edwards (1996), presents the individual with a particular and limiting set of expectations and rules of conduct.

The career helping process also has a 'professional' dimension, whereby the individual is presented with particular expectations and rules which are determined by the espoused theories of the helper. Karasu (1984) have identified over 480 theoretical frameworks for helping individuals.

These can be placed into the following broad categories: psychodynamic; social-psychological; humanistic; cognitive-behavioural; trait–factor; and integrative (Cormier and Cormier, 1991). Although career helping frameworks can be found in each of these categories, there is evidence to suggest that a narrow range is used in practice, certainly in the UK (Kidd et al., 1994; 1996).

However, despite the plethora of theoretical orientations, there is also evidence to suggest that there is a lack of integration between theory and the practice of career helping (Kidd et al., 1994; 1996). More specifically, evidence has been found to indicate that the activities of advice and information giving predominate in career helping interactions (Stacey and Mignot, 2000). The reasons for this are numerous and complex and relate to both the 'managerial' and the 'professional' dimensions of the 'career' helping process.

For example, the notion of a 'managerial' discourse certainly resonates with the increasingly ambitious targets set initially by the 'focusing' of the careers service (DfEE, 1998b; 1999b), and subsequently by the Connexions initiative (DfEE, 2000a; 2000c). The following is an example:

> The nature and length of [the interview] must depend upon the level of Careers Service input required. Those who are well-informed and clear in their thinking need only short interviews. Those who are ill-informed, unclear or at risk need more help. This can include low achievers, those unlikely to do well at GCSE yet considering 'A' levels, and some of the academically able who have not thought through the implications of their post-16 choices. Teachers should be asked to refer those they are concerned about for early interview. Some may need two or more interviews. (DfEE, 1998b: 10)

As an example of 'managerial' discourse, this specification clearly relies on a rational notion of 'self': the individual viewed as a rational decision maker and processor of information. It also makes particular demands of the practitioner: the specification clearly implies that the career helping interaction will be concerned with diagnosing the 'realism' of the client's thinking. The notion of diagnosis, in turn, implies a medical model of intervention which has been seen as problematic in the context of career helping (Gothard and Mignot, 1999). This is because career helping is not a scientific enterprise, as evidenced by the continuing concern surrounding the validity and reliability of psychometric testing (CRE, 1992). Furthermore, as the DfEE specification given above clearly indicates, the diagnosis of realism is a relative rather than an objective exercise. In other words the practitioner is required to engage in a complex balancing act: the distribution of limited resources requires a judgement of how realistic one individual is in relation to other individuals. On this basis, the medical model of intervention provides a pragmatic response to managerial imperatives. It is also highly sympathetic to a 'professional' discourse founded upon the accumulation and application of knowledge (Payne and Edwards, 1996).

In the context of career helping, practitioners accumulate and apply professional knowledge of the 'opportunity structure'. This includes knowledge of national and local education, training and labour markets. Clarke (1994) has suggested that career helpers develop increasingly sophisticated cognitive maps of the opportunity structure and that this process is mediated by their professional socialisation. In other words the practitioner's cognitive map of opportunities is not value-free. Rather it is influenced by the expectations of opportunity providers – employers, schools, training organisations, etc. Clarke (1994) has also suggested that career helpers use their cognitive maps as a diagnostic framework, allowing the practitioner to make 'shortcuts' and to process the interaction more efficiently. On this basis, the practitioner's cognitive map of opportunities provides the means to construct various outcomes for the client. More specifically, the application of professional knowledge within a medical model of career helping serves three key purposes. First, it provides a set of criteria by which to measure the realism of the client's career ideas. Second, should circumstances require an unproblematic outcome, professional knowledge provides the means to construct a 'realistic', 'low-risk' client. Third, the application of professional knowledge allows the practitioner to conform to the unspoken expectations of a client that has anticipated the rules of the medical model. These key purposes are augmented and reinforced by mechanisms such as the career action plan. In 1998 it was a DfEE requirement that career action plans recorded the following information:

- the client's current situation
- their decisions about clear educational/training/occupational goals
- the rationale behind those decisions
- the next steps to reach their goals and timing. (DfEE, 1998b)

Given the prescriptive nature of the career action plan, the practitioner may be bound still further to the medical model of intervention which, by placing professional knowledge and diagnosis centre stage, shifts the emphasis of the career helping interaction towards the provision of advice and information. This in turn de-emphasises the counselling dimension of career helping which features strongly in the initial training of practitioners (Ali and Graham, 1996; Gothard and Mignot, 1999). One possible implication of this is that the client ultimately has limited access to support in the formulation and development of career ideas and in the reconciliation of career decisions. Many career helpers will not lose the irony of this position, given that a considerable amount of their professional training is dedicated to the application of counselling skills in career helping contexts.

It is the author's view that the 'managerial' discourse identified in the foregoing analysis can be regarded as immutable; the 'ambitious' targets set for the Connexions service is evidence for this claim. In addition, the medical model of intervention is a concomitant of the managerial view of the 'rational' client; indeed, medical metaphors such as 'general practitioner' and 'triage' have already been associated with the role of the Connexions personal adviser (DfEE, 2000d). However, the 'professional' discourse identified in the foregoing analysis can, in contrast, be regarded as mutable. For example, at the time of writing there is considerable uncertainty about the professional identity of the Connexions personal adviser. This in turn reflects the lack of clarity on what will constitute the professional knowledge of this new role. The author suggests that this uncertainty provides a discursive space within which to redress the balance of support offered to young people at the point of intervention. In other words, there is currently an opportunity to reconstruct a 'professional' discourse that provides clients with access to the range of career helping activities as defined by UDACE (1986) and SCAGES (1993). The next section will therefore return to the fundamental question: 'What do we mean by career helping?'

What do we mean by career helping?

In this section, the possibilities for what might constitute career helping will be explored. So far a simple classification has been used to define the nature of career helping; it is now necessary to provide a more sophisticated definition.

According to UDACE (1986) career helping encompasses the following activities: informing; advising; counselling; assessing; enabling; advocating; feeding back. In order to emphasise the educational dimension of career helping, SCAGES (1993) added the following to the UDACE definition: teaching; managing; innovating/systems change. 'Teaching' is defined by SCAGES as:

> providing a planned and systematic progression of learner-centred experiences to enable learners to acquire knowledge, skills and competencies related to making personal, educational and career decisions and transitions. (1993: 37)

It is the author's view that the UDACE/SCAGES definition of career helping provides a useful framework for thinking about how individuals might be helped in the light of the new 'career'. More importantly, the definition provides the stimulus to think beyond the dichotomy of careers guidance versus job advice. This is necessary if any meaningful discussion is to take place around how all individuals, irrespective of where they are located within the labour market, might be helped in the context of 'career'. However, it is also the author's view that the reference to 'teaching' should be changed to 'teaching and learning' and 'enabling' changed to 'enabling inclusion'. These changes provide even greater congruence between the UDACE/SCAGES definition and contemporary issues related to 'lifelong learning' and 'social exclusion'. For example, the amended definition raises immediate questions about: (1) the nature of learning and how career helping might support individual learning; (2) how career helping might enable individuals and groups to achieve a greater degree of social inclusion. It is important to acknowledge that both of these questions have been addressed in the past by theoreticians and practitioners. The former question has been addressed explicitly by both developmental and behavioural 'career' theorists (e.g. Mitchell and Krumboltz, 1996; Super, 1990) and most recently by Law (1996a). The latter question, which has been debated within a wide range of helping professions (Bimrose, 1993; Halmos, 1974; Lago and Thompson, 1996; Smail, 1991; Watts, 1996a), relates to the proposition that 'career' helpers need a means of working satisfactorily with both individuals and social structures. The positioning of 'career' at the interfaces between the citizen and the state, and between the individual and society, means that career helping is inevitably a political activity (Watts, 1996b). Thus, many 'career' helpers are presented with the recurrent dilemma not only of reconciling client-centred values with socio-economic interests, but also of finding ways of resisting oppression through anti-oppressive practice (Thompson, 1997; Wrench, 1992). In this regard, Bimrose has described three approaches to counselling in terms of how these relate and respond to social context: 'individualist', 'integrationist' and 'structuralist' (1993: 162). Bimrose contends that the structuralist approach has yet to be clearly conceptualised and articulated; indeed this approach suggests 'the requirement for the development of a different theoretical base on which practice might be based' (1993: 162). In similar vein, Fitzgerald and Betz have suggested that the theories of career development currently available 'lack a systematic explanation of the role of structural and cultural factors in shaping individual vocational behavior' (1994: 107). Lago and Thompson (1996) are clear about why this is the case. They assert that individual helping is inevitably grounded not only in the discipline of psychology, but also in the notion of pathology. As such, it is of critical importance that helpers develop 'a systematic structural understanding of society' (1996: 16).

So, given the wider definition of both 'career' and career helping, what sort of helping frameworks are available to practitioners? The next section will provide an overview of those most commonly used in the UK.

Career helping frameworks

According to Kidd (1996b) there are four distinct frameworks for career helping to be found in the UK. These are as follows:

- *Trait–factor* approaches to career helping became popular in the post-war period. This approach assumes that both individuals (in terms of interests, attributes etc.) and occupations (in terms of skill requirements etc.) can be assessed and therefore *matched*. These assumptions provide the basis for the design of psychometric instruments. In terms of interviewing strategies, the 'seven-point plan' devised by Rodger (1952) became particularly influential within the UK and remains to this day a feature of contemporary career helping practice.

- *Goal-directed* approaches to career helping include both Egan's (1994) 'skilled helper' model and those derived from behavioural psychology – Krumboltz's 'social learning theory of career decision making' being the most well known (see Mitchell and Krumboltz, 1996). Goal-directed approaches emphasise behavioural change and action: here the client is helped to identify 'blind spots' in their thinking and to formulate goals and courses of action based on new perspectives of what is possible and achievable.

- *Person-centred* approaches to career helping draw significantly from the work of Rogers (1951). This approach stresses the nature of the *relationship* between the helper and client, together with the *values* held by the helper. Central to the person-centred approach are the *core conditions* of 'respect', 'genuineness' and 'empathy'. These conditions are both necessary to achieving an understanding of the client's internal frame of reference, and *sufficient* in terms of promoting positive benefits for the client.

- *Developmental* approaches to career helping acknowledge that there are a number of developmental stages or tasks that the client engages with in the process of becoming 'vocationally mature' or aware. On this basis career helping practitioners (including career educators) need to tailor their helping interventions to the level of career development achieved by the client. The work of Super (1990) and more recently Law (1996a) have been particularly influential here.

Kidd (1996b) acknowledges that the four categories described above, whilst being fundamentally distinctive, do overlap. Furthermore, in their survey of career helpers, Kidd et al. (1994; 1996) found that person-centred and developmental approaches were most popular. Egan's (1994) 'skilled helper' model was also cited as a useful practical framework.

The research undertaken by Kidd et al. (1994) remains to this day the most recent and comprehensive survey of career helping practice. Their survey investigated the level of awareness amongst career helpers of a range of theoretical perspectives and the degree to which theory is integrated with career helping practice. However, the survey cannot be regarded as representative, either in terms of the sample population of career helpers surveyed, or in terms of the range of theoretical perspectives presented in the survey questionnaire. The latter is understandable, particularly given the considerable number of helping orientations quoted in the literature – over 480 being the most recent estimate (Lago and Thompson, 1996). To make sense of such a large number of helping orientations certainly requires a category system of some sort. This in turn inevitably gives primacy to particular orientations whilst de-emphasising others. It is the author's view that any procedure for categorising career helping orientations should begin with the question of *epistemology* rather than *ontology*, i.e. the *world view* that informs theory construction rather than the theory itself.

Competing world views of career helping

How we go about providing career help is, like any other activity, inevitably dependent upon our world view, or 'epistemology'. In acknowledging the difficulty of the term, Griffiths has described epistemology as:

> a set of questions and issues about knowledge: what it is, how we get it, how we recognise it, how it relates to truth, how it is entangled with power. (1998: 5)

Furthermore, at the centre of any question related to epistemology is a set of assumptions about the nature of 'self' (Popkewitz, 1991; Goncalves, 1995). The various epistemological perspectives that underpin career helping will now be considered.

Positivism

There is evidence to suggest that career development theory and career helping practices continue to be strongly influenced by a positivist epistemology (Brown, 1996; Collin and Young, 1986; Fitzgerald and Betz, 1994). Indeed, with the exception of the person-centred approach, each of the career helping frameworks identified in the previous section can be located within the positivist tradition. Positivism utilises a *rational* sense of 'self' which assumes a relatively stable sense of identity. Hodkinson et al. (1996) have suggested that a 'rational' notion of self is attractive to policy makers because it assumes that all individuals are capable of processing information and making career decisions 'rationally' and autonomously. This in turn provides a justification for the use of trait–factor methods of practice which, in the short term, are highly expedient and 'measurable', particularly when resources are scarce. However, positivism is currently under challenge by theorists and researchers who view the rational 'self' as no longer tenable, given the nature of contemporary career development and the need for alternative approaches to career helping practice (Gelatt, 1989).

Constructivism

As an alternative to positivism, constructivism is attracting considerable interest from those who wish to acknowledge the ambiguity, uncertainty and inconsistency of individual career development. Contextualist perspectives which adopt a hermeneutic approach to inquiry as a means of interpreting individual 'careers' in context (Young and Collin, 1992; Young et al. 1996) are also evident here. Contextualism places particular emphasis on socio-ecological systems in the process of interpreting and understanding the nature of career. Within this general trend can be found the work of Payne and Edwards (1996). In questioning the validity of impartial guidance Payne and Edwards suggest that a rational autonomous 'self' underpins the practice of impartiality which, they contend, maintains oppressive social systems through the act of 'omission' (Thompson, 1997). As an alternative, Payne and Edwards (1994) utilise a version of 'self' drawn loosely from constructivism to support their proposal for *partial* guidance. This proposal invites career helpers to work to counter the false consciousness of clients based on the acknowledgement that 'career' is a classed, racialised and gendered construct.

Goncalves (1995) has provided an important reappraisal of the constructivist world view on helping. Goncalves focuses on the use of narrative in psychotherapy in order to contrast the constructivist paradigm with two positivist helping orientations: behavioural and cognitive-behavioural. Goncalves (1995) contends that behavioural helping orientations are concerned solely with *objectivity*, and that cognitive-behavioural orientations are primarily concerned with *subjectivity*. Goncalves then provides a further alternative to helping that transcends the subject–object distinction – a *narrative* orientation that emphasises *projectivity*:

> With human beings there is more than a narrative. There is a definite narrator, someone who moves between the position of the subject and object of the story construction. In the process of writing their tales, humans skilfully elude the distinction between themselves as objects and themselves as subjects; they turn into 'projects', that is, objects thrown forth into a process of continuous, endless, and somehow unpredictable movement. (1995: 197)

It is the author's view that Goncalves's notion of projectivity, that is 'the continuous construction and deconstruction of human projects' (1995: 202), provides the basis for new ways of conceptualising the career helping process. Following Goncalves, the next section will describe a framework for career helping which focuses on the narratives that individuals construct as they engage in their life projects.

A narrative approach to career helping

Law (1996a) has recently elaborated a new theory on career development – 'career learning theory'. In so doing, Law's principal aim was to inform the development of the careers education curriculum. However, Law (1996a) has also acknowledged that the theory can be applied as a framework for career helping. Career learning theory suggests that effective career learning is dependent upon learners developing the following capacities: 'sensing', 'sifting', 'focusing' and 'understanding'. More specifically, this involves helping learners:

1 To gather and map out information on 'career'; this also includes helping learners to construct narratives that take account of time, place and space.
2 To compare and contrast elements of their 'career' narratives through identifying and applying personal *constructs* (e.g. 'high status, low status'); this also includes helping learners to share their personal constructs with others in order to make links with public 'career' *concepts* (e.g. 'arts', 'business' etc.).
3 To engage in encounters with other people's views on 'career' and to express their own views.
4 To understand how their developing 'career' narrative links with the wider socio-economic context; this also includes helping learners to *visualise* future events and to anticipate the consequences of different courses of action.

According to Law (1996a) these four learning stages are both progressive and cyclical: the description and organisation of 'career' material provides the foundation upon which to prioritise and visualise preferred 'career' scenarios. These stages are also highly congruent with what has been termed a *hermeneutic* approach to career helping (Collin and Young, 1986; Gothard and Mignot, 1999; Mignot, 2000a; Young and Collin, 1988; 1992). Career helping informed by hermeneutic principles can be differentiated from other models of practice in the following ways. First, the emphasis is on *interpretation* rather than assessment or diagnosis. In this sense the client becomes a *participant* rather than a passive recipient of another's expertise. Second, it is acknowledged that both participants bring differing points of view to the interaction, thereby ensuring the opportunity for 'critical feedback' (Sullivan, 1990: 117). This emphasises the iterative nature of the career helping process which relies upon both collaboration and negotiation between the participants involved. Third, the nature of the relationship between the participants is founded upon the Rogerian values of respect, genuineness and empathy. This emphasises that the partici-pants should strive for an empathic understanding of the other's point of view, whilst having the freedom to express their own views; mutual and unconditional respect is a necessary condition for a helping relationship such as this. Gothard and Mignot (1999) have recently formalised the link between hermeneutics and guidance practice founded upon the person-centred tradition. Their hermeneutic model of guidance deploys career learning theory as an interpretive framework, whereby the four stages of 'sensing', 'sifting', 'focusing' and 'understanding' are used as a means of 'scaffolding' (Vygotsky, 1978) the career learning of participants. This framework, expressed as the mnemonic FIRST, will be described in detail in the following section.

The FIRST framework

In 1982 Tol Bedford developed the FIRST framework as a means of evaluating career helping interactions. FIRST was used initially by Employment Department Careers Service inspectors, and subsequently by some Careers Service providers as a quality assurance framework for guidance interviewing. Most recently it has appeared as a tool for measuring the careers education learning outcomes of students (DfEE, 1999a). The mnemonic FIRST is as follows:

- *Focus* To what extent has the client narrowed down their options?
- *Information* How well informed is the client?
- *Realism* How realistic is the client given their own capabilities and the constraints of the labour market?
- *Scope* How aware is the client of the range of options available?
- *Tactics* Does the client know how to put their plans into action?

As the above indicates, FIRST represents a set of questions that can be used within the career helping process. However, these questions are not just about *outcomes* but also about starting points, i.e. the *current position* of the client as s/he engages with the career helping process. According to Bedford (1982) the effectiveness of the career helping process can be 'measured' by comparing current position with outcome. This is demonstrated diagrammatically in Figure 3.1. Bedford also suggested that the five dimensions of FIRST are interrelated: taken together they provide an indication of the *vocational awareness* of the client. On this basis FIRST has been defined as a developmental model (Kidd, 1996b) whereby developing scope (awareness of a range of options) goes hand in hand with achieving focus (narrowing down options). The provision of information and tactical awareness is seen as having a dual role in helping to develop scope *and* to achieve focus. As with all developmental models, the task for the career helper is to identify the level of the client's vocational development; in so doing both helper and client gain an improved understanding of how to proceed. Bedford (1982) used the term *diagnosis* in this context, a medical term which, as we have seen, has connotations for the notion of treatment and cure etc.

Gothard and Mignot (1999), in revisiting the FIRST framework, concluded that its developmental orientation was not sufficiently explicit for the purposes of career helping. They subsequently proposed an integrated framework drawing significantly on the developmental orientation of Law's (1996a) career learning theory. Table 3.1 outlines the initial integration of the FIRST framework with the career learning repertoires identified by Law (1996a).

The arrangement of career learning theory and FIRST described in linear terms in Table 3.1 provides the initial step towards an integration of Law's and Bedford's work. However, this arrangement does not make explicit the

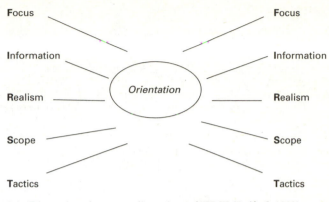

Figure 3.1 *Diagnosis and progress dimensions of FIRST (Bedford, 1982)*

Table 3.1 *Linking career learning theory and the FIRST framework*

Career learning repertoires	FIRST
Sensing Gathering information and assembling sequences	*Information* How well informed is the client about the careers options s/he has in mind?
Sifting Using concepts and making comparisons	*Scope* How aware is the client of the range of options available?
Focusing Dealing with points of view and taking one's own view	*Focus* How far has the client narrowed down options?
Understanding Developing explanations and anticipating consequences.	*Realism and tactics* How realistic is the client? To what extent has the client worked out the practical steps necessary to achieve career objectives?

cyclical and progressive features of career learning theory. Furthermore, and for the reasons already explained in this chapter, it is important to distance this work from the medical model of practice. As such, careful attention needs to be given to the 'realism' dimension of FIRST which has strong positivist connotations. For example, the issue of 'realism' raises an immediate question around who becomes the arbiter of what is 'realistic' – the career helper, the client, other parties?

It is appropriate and necessary at this point to provide a case example.

A case example: Jav

Jav: Computer programming is for me – information technology – it's where
           things are going in the future, we're all using them. I surf the net with
           my mates all the time – and my brother's doing a course – he says it's
           really good. Anyway, what I want in the future is plenty of money – a
           decent job, good clothes, a flash car.
Helper: What is it about computers that you like, Jav?
Jav: Computers is hi-tech, it's fast you know – the latest machines work really
           quick – you can get loads of extras, over and above the basic. You can
           be mobile too – any time, anywhere – work from home, on the train – be
           your own boss – no one looking over your shoulder.
Helper: Is there anything that you've said that would be really important for
           you in the future?
Jav: No one looking over your shoulder – that would be it. I don't know, it's
           always been the same – someone's always got to have a dig at you. It was
           like that at school – I never got it right. When I'm left to get on with it I
           feel good, more relaxed.

In applying FIRST as a career helping framework for working with Jav, it
is clear that the category 'realism' is particularly problematic. Consider the
following question:

> How *realistic* is Jav – in relation both to his own abilities and to the constraints
> of the market?

If, as Bedford (1982) has suggested, FIRST represents the professional
constructs of guidance practitioners, then the uncertain, idiosyncratic and
ambiguous statements that Jav has expressed may be obscured through
applying this construct of 'realism' (Collin, 1997; Gelatt, 1989; Law, 1996a).
This would suggest that FIRST needs significant amendment in order to
provide the basis for a model of practice.

The first amendment acknowledges that 'realism' is a counter-productive
term, lending itself to a premature judgement by the career helper on behalf
of the client. A visual demonstration of this adjustment is thus:

FIRST → FIrST

The second amendment relates to the *general* and *specific* statements that are
contained in the client's narrative. In Jav's case, examples include:

- *General* 'No one looking over your shoulder'; 'when I'm left to get on
  with it I feel good, more relaxed.'
- *Specific* 'Computer programming'; 'information technology'.

If such general *and* specific statements are viewed as central to the career
helping dialogue, then this would suggest that the 'focus' and 'scope'
categories have primary significance within FIrST. Therefore, if 'focus' and
'scope' are expressed differently – i.e. in terms of *narrowing* and *widening*,

specific and *general* – this would form a natural relationship, or dynamic, from which a framework for career helping practice can be drawn. However, there is a further consideration that FIrST does not address. If it is acknowledged that the career helping interaction takes place in a specific context, and in part addresses future contexts or possible scenarios (Neimeyer, 1992), then it is important to attend to the process and effects of *anticipation*, i.e. how the client anticipates future scenarios will affect what s/he feels, thinks, says and does in the present (Kelly, 1955). This consideration acknowledges that all helping discussions are grounded in context. It also acknowledges that the client may be anticipating a number of contexts in 'career' terms which may form the basis for goal-directed action. The relative significance given by the client to these anticipated contexts is an important key both to a greater understanding of the client's view and to negotiating the context/contract for the helping interaction.

These considerations – removing 'realism' as an explicit professional construct, emphasising the relationship between 'focus' and 'scope', and acknowledging the critical process of anticipation – provide the means to reconfigure FIrST as a model for practice that may be more adequate for the purposes of career helping in the post-bureaucratic era.

It is appropriate, at this point, to provide a conceptual overview of the FIrST framework in diagrammatic form. Figure 3.2 also incorporates the various career learning capacities expressed by Law (1996a). In Figure 3.2, 'focus' and 'scope' are arranged as the primary dynamic of the framework and invite the career helper to attend to the specific and to the general – to the narrowing and the widening of the client's career thinking. 'Scope' serves to accommodate the infinite variety of constructs a person might express as significant: in Jav's case these included 'no one looking over your shoulder'; 'when I'm left to get on with it I feel good, more relaxed', which are reflected in his 'focus' on 'computer programming' and 'information technology' as he anticipates the prospect of work.

'Information' and 'tactics' provide the point of demarcation between the *private* and the *public* domain: they represent the sources of information and tactical knowledge that are available to the client, both formally and informally (e.g. through library databases, the Internet, friends, relations etc.). This point of demarcation between the private and the public has a dual purpose – serving to promote both 'scope' and 'focus' in the client's career thinking.

Used in combination, the categories of FIrST can, at a heuristic level, help to interpret and understand the degree to which the client might be able to *implement* their ideas. In Jav's case, we might understand him to be in a 'position of scope': despite focusing on the 'computer programming' and 'information technology', Jav expresses little *publicly* held information and tactical knowledge about work in this field. However Jav is actively engaged with informal sources of information (specifically his brother) and he has perceptions of 'computer programming' that are personally significant, important and influential for him.

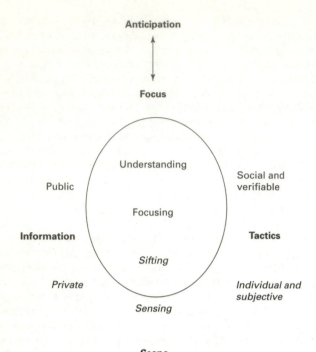

Figure 3.2 *The FIrST framework*

So, in summary, FIrST asks the participants of the career helping interaction three initial and fundamental questions:

1 What future scenarios is the client *anticipating*?
2 What are the *specific* ('focus') and general ('scope') statements the client makes in anticipating these scenarios?
3 What sources of *publicly* held 'information' and 'tactical' knowledge is the client engaging with?

Thus, the FIrST framework provides a provisional map for an *interpretation* of the client's story. However, by incorporating career learning theory, the framework also provides an opportunity to develop this interpretation whereby a greater *understanding* of the client's career narrative can be achieved.

According to career learning theory, career learning involves the *progressive* development of an individual's capacities to 'sense', 'sift' and 'focus', leading to 'understanding'. This progression also describes the movement from the private to the public world, from personally held constructs to publicly held *concepts*. Another feature of career learning is the nature of 'sensing' as an activity: career learning theory acknowledges the presence and validity of *impressionistic* information such as touch, taste and smell. These features would suggest a high degree of congruence between career learning theory and FIrST.

For example, some of what Jav expressed could be understood, in career learning terms, as 'focusing' ('dealing with other points of view'): Jav's brother is doing a course in 'computer programming' and says 'it's really good'. Jav expresses little else in specific terms about 'computer programming' and 'information technology': he offers few explanations of what might be involved, and there is little to suggest his view of the 'anticipated consequences' of doing or pursuing this as a specific choice in the social world. Jav's capacity for understanding, in career learning terms, has yet to be developed.

However, Jav has a considerable amount to say about what he generally associates with 'computer programming': here 'computer programming' functions as a public concept that reflects what Jav finds subjectively and privately significant and meaningful at the present time. By attending to, and acknowledging, Jav's 'sensing' and 'sifting' of constructs and concepts, the career helping interaction might help Jav to develop his career narrative in novel ways. How might this be achieved in practice?

In his exposition of career learning theory, Law (1996a) invites career helpers to consider an eclectic blend of techniques. For example, by using the 'laddering' and 'pyramiding' techniques associated with personal construct psychology (Pope and Keen, 1981) Jav could be helped to antici- pate 'why' or 'in what way' his constructs might have significance and impact in career terms. For example, 'in what other ways' or 'in what other circumstances' might Jav experience 'no one looking over your shoulder' and 'feeling good, more relaxed'? In so doing, Jav could be helped to elaborate his narrative or storyline (McLeod, 1996) from one or more of his constructs. Through the development of his narrative it may be possible for Jav to apprehend alternative semblances of meaning, in career terms, from his thoughts, feelings and actions (Young and Collin, 1992), e.g. helping Jav to construct a story where 'no one is looking over his shoulder' and where he is 'feeling good and relaxed'; attending to scenes, people, places and new plot lines.

These general principles for narrative construction will now be devel- oped by looking again at the FIrST framework. Figure 3.3 provides an analogue model of the FIrST framework: it is presented in the familiar form of the iceberg. Using the iceberg analogy, we can view the personal and private world of the individual as being 'below the surface': the extent of the submerged part of the iceberg can be sensed but not clearly defined. The iceberg also has a visible, terrestrial part, which can be viewed as being in the public and social world. However, the terrestrial part of the iceberg is exposed to the elements: it changes shape over time dependent on the prevailing conditions. In contrast, the submerged part is relatively stable over time, irrespective of the conditions above the surface.

Focus

Understanding

(providing explanations and
anticipating consequences)

Focusing

(taking a personal view and
dealing with others' points of view)

Sifting

Constructs and concepts

(roles, traits, labels,
contrasts and similarities)

Sensing

Narrative base

(intuition, impressions, describing
experiences and feelings,
story-telling with plot lines
and characters)

Scope

Figure 3.3   *The iceberg model*

The iceberg analogy can be translated into career learning terms in a variety of ways. For example, our values, beliefs and sources of motivation tend to be relatively constant in comparison to the specific activities that we undertake. Simply put, there are many ways to pursue what we sense to be important and significant in our lives: the jobs that we do are just the tip of the iceberg! Thus, some clients seeking help with 'career' may benefit from working with their career helper at a level below the surface, at the base of the iceberg, in order to explore alternative 'career' narratives.

For those clients wishing to work above the surface, at the tip of the iceberg, career learning theory would suggest that the primary goal is that of enabling 'understanding'. Law (1996a) defines this career learning capacity in terms of the client 'developing explanations' and 'anticipating consequences'. It is here that the *political* dimension of the client's narrative gains significance. As Mair suggests: 'All tellings are political in the sense that they reflect the hidden structure of power and privilege in which the speaker and the audience are located' (1989: 9).

Drawing from Freire's (1973) notion of 'conscientisation', career helpers could enable their clients to develop a *critical* view of 'career'. For example, in developing their explanatory career narratives, clients could gain an understanding of the racialised, classed and gendered nature of the labour market. This proposition is aligned to Payne and Edwards's (1996) view that *partial* career helping has greater legitimacy than impartial approaches which are implicitly political. This proposition also implies that career helpers need a *critical* understanding of social structures and systems (Lago and Thompson, 1996; Mignot, 2000b).

Returning to the iceberg analogy, the following section will describe two contrasting techniques that are designed to help individuals to work at the 'below the surface' level – to sense and sift new possibilities for 'career'.

Helping to construct 'career' narratives

In what follows two specific techniques for narrative construction will be briefly outlined. Throughout this section the term 'participant' will be used to denote the collaborative nature of the narrative construction process. The first technique, 'role models', has been developed most recently by Cochran (1997).

Role models

The notion of 'role modelling' has been addressed by a number of 'career' theorists and indeed is a central feature of Law's (1996a) work on career learning. As a narrative construct, an individual 'role model' can be seen as a central character in an unfolding storyline. The participant of the career helping process is first asked to think about a particular character in their lives who is significant to them. The word 'character' is used here to denote that role models potentially include fictional characters, e.g. from soap operas and films, and even cartoon characters. The participant is then asked to tell the story of how, where and when their role model became significant to them. This includes asking the participant to describe their role model in detail (this procedure may need to be repeated if the participant identifies more than one role model). Questions such as how the participant is similar and different from the model can be explored: this is an important feature of the narrative process as the participant's role model may be one that portrays ways of being that the participant wishes to avoid. During this process it is important to establish the context of the participant's life when the character became the model. Given the client's context at a particular time, a role model can portray ways of being in order to manage difficulties or achieve a particular goal.

This 'below the surface' technique is designed to help the participant to review their lived experiences as a basis for constructing and reconstructing their personal narrative. The second technique, which involves the use of visual material, is based on the same principle.

Using visual methods to construct a narrative

The author (Mignot, 2000a) has developed the following visual methods for use with individuals participating in the career helping process.

First, participants are invited to construct a 'photograph album' of aspects of their lives that are significant to them in 'career' terms. By taking photographs of people, places, events, objects etc., participants have the opportunity to construct a personal map of any number of images. In so doing participants are 'sifting' images: their choices in terms of what, where and when to photograph will be guided by, and will in turn demonstrate, the way in which they make comparisons and apply concepts. This will also be influenced by the briefing given to participants at the start of the activity. For example, participants can be invited to construct a photographic record of 'ideal' and 'less than ideal' career scenarios: here contrast is an in-built feature of the activity. The photographs provide the basis for interpreting 'career'. This interpretation is undertaken by identifying the themes that are embedded within the participants' visual narratives. This is achieved by inviting the participants to describe and manipulate their photographic images in ways that are meaningful to them. In so doing, participants are encouraged to engage in the following procedures:

1 As a general principle, the participant is asked to provide a descriptive account of each photograph. This descriptive act reveals the context of the photograph which in turn guides the emerging narrative: for example, a building in a photograph might be described as 'modern and colourful'. In so doing, description is displaced by interpretation which is then elaborated in the form of narrative.
2 More specifically, the participant is asked to relate each photograph to the context of 'career'. This can be achieved through 'laddering' type questions, e.g. 'Given that we're discussing how you see your future, why did you decide to take a photograph of this building?'

It is here that the photograph functions as a metaphor in that it fuses the context of 'career' with the emerging narrative. The photograph also contains innumerable parts each of which might be 'read' differently. This recognises the potential for photographs to both disguise and reveal meaning. In essence, the interpretive process aims to develop amongst the viewers an empathic understanding not of the photograph, but of the meanings that they construct and reconstruct as they interpret the photographic image.

Second, narrative construction is facilitated yet further through the use of 'montage'. The 'montage' technique involves encouraging participants to manipulate their photographs in ways that are significant to them: turning some face down, placing some in linear sequence to denote the passage of time or the pursuit of goals, placing some in a group to indicate a relationship, placing some apart to express difference or contrast, etc. The montage can subsequently be reconstructed in various ways, for example:

1 Moving, removing or adding photographs in reference to an alternative context, e.g. 'If this represented your future rather than your past, would you change the montage in any way?'; 'If we took this picture out of the montage, would it tell a different story?'
2 asking the participant to consider missing photographs, e.g. 'If this montage became "your future", what other pictures would you need?'; 'There are no pictures of people here – why do you think that is?'

Third, narrative construction and reconstruction can be continued through the use of 'mural'. The 'mural' technique involves creating a wall mural from participants' photographs; this might include the use of collage, painting and drawing. The construction of the mural draws from the processes of 'montage': new relationships, sequences etc. emerge as participants make decisions about their composition. 'Mural' is a group activity, designed to make public the private constructions of individual participants.

As this chapter has already indicated, narrative methods require that special attention is given to the nature of the relationship between the participants of the career helping process, i.e. that the Rogerian core values of respect, genuineness and empathy need to be present as participants engage in narrative construction. In this regard, the use of narrative methods would seem to have a high degree of congruence with the practice of mentoring – a practice which is central to the Connexions strategy (DfEE, 2000a; Youth Justice Board, 2000). Furthermore, narrative methods deployed within a person-centred relationship also have potential within the context of the supervision, i.e. through the process of supervision both parties could be helped to elaborate their practitioner narratives. The role and function of supervision for career helpers will now be discussed.

A final note: supervision and career helping

As many writers have stated, the primary purpose of supervision is to promote and protect the best interests of the client (BAC, 1988; Hawkins and Shohet, 1989; Hess, 1980). According to Hawkins and Shohet (1989), supervision can be seen to have three functions. The first is an *educative* function whereby the supervisee is helped to develop a greater under-standing not only of their clients, but also of their own reactions and responses as they engage in the helping process. The educative function of supervision also provides the supervisee with an opportunity to reflect on the nature of their interventions with clients and to explore other ways of working. The second is a *supportive* function whereby time is provided for supervisees to express their feelings about their work. The third is a *managerial* function which ensures that supervisees are meeting the required standards of the profession/organisation.

Clearly, there is potential here for a mismatch of expectations. This in turn indicates the critical importance of having a clear contract for

Table 3.2 *Potential activities for supervision*

- To provide regular space for the supervisees to reflect upon the content and process of their work (educational)
- To develop understanding and skills within the work (educational)
- To receive information and another perspective concerning one's work (educational/supportive)
- To receive both content and process feedback (educational/supportive)
- To be validated and supported both as a person and as a worker (supportive)
- To ensure that as a person and as a worker one is not left to carry, unnecessarily, difficulties, problems and projections alone (supportive)
- To have space to explore and express personal feelings that may be brought up by the work (managerial/supportive)
- To plan and utilise their personal and professional resources better (managerial/supportive)
- To be proactive rather than reactive (managerial/supportive)
- To ensure quality of work (managerial)

Source: Hawkins and Shohet, 1989

supervision. Table 3.2 provides a range of activities that might provide the basis for such a contract. As the table clearly indicates, good supervision can be described as a carefully planned and negotiated activity. Furthermore, it requires particular qualities from the supervisor. These include empathy, understanding, unconditional positive regard, genuineness, warmth and self-disclosure, flexibility, concern, attentiveness and openness (Carifio and Hess, 1987). Clearly there is a high degree of congruence between these qualities and career helping grounded in the person-centred tradition. In this respect, good supervision has a natural affinity with good career helping. Finally, as will become clear in Chapter 8, good supervision is essential to effective anti-oppressive practice.

4

GROUP WORK: GUIDANCE IN A GROUP SETTING

Traditionally the one-to-one guidance conversation or interview has been the central plank of most careers professionals' repertoire, the skill and process by which they felt they were known. To tell a careers adviser that they were no good at guidance interviewing would be to challenge their professional identity.

Working with groups, also part of the traditional training programme, has been a long-established form of intervention in careers education and guidance (CEG), especially in secondary schools. However, according to Bysshe et al. (1997: 4), in 1995 a DfEE-commissioned survey found that only 24 per cent of Year 11 and 12 per cent of Year 10 pupils had been involved in such sessions. The value and importance of group work have been seen as distinctly secondary, to the point where some careers advisers would say that 'guidance' could only be delivered by a one-to-one interaction. It is not surprising, then, to find that very little has been written about group work as a tool in careers education and guidance. A search of the literature reveals only a handful of references, by comparison with the long list of items about the individual interview. It is also much more difficult to define: there is a range of interventions involving anything from four or five participants up to several hundred in a school hall or conference centre, all of which might at times be referred to as 'group work'.

Twenty or thirty years ago careers advisers might interact with groups only via the 'school talk', typically an address to a large group of pupils approaching their ultimate or penultimate year of compulsory schooling, held in the school hall, perhaps after assembly, to explain what the careers service had to offer them, and how they could access it individually. This had all the hallmarks of a public presentation, and generally allowed for relatively little interaction with the audience.

Even as little as 10 years ago, the decision as to whether careers advisers used group interventions and to what extent and for what purposes might be determined as much by individual practitioners' preferences as by any policy of the Careers Service. There was little or no guidance from central government until the *Careers Service Planning Guidance* for 1996–7 specified that all students must receive three small group sessions in Years 9 and 10 and one session in Year 11. A small group work session 'was then defined as one where guidance and help to individuals can be given in a group, up to and including 10 individuals', drawing a distinction between this and the purpose of larger groups which aimed to 'provide the opportunity to give information to people' (Bysshe et al., 1997: 8)

In the survey just quoted, it was further evident that 'in the survey areas, Group Work delivery is mainly in class size groups, with the majority being in the context of Careers Education or PSE lessons' (1997: 14) because doing it in other contexts was logistically difficult, few schools being able to offer the curriculum time. Group work targets were being met by a motley variety of means from short inputs at registration or in tutorial time, to team interventions by careers advisers when working with a single school at a special event where the normal timetable had been suspended for the occasion. It might even be subcontracted to school staff through service level or partnership agreements between schools and the local Careers Service. All this time, however, there had also been other activities outside school altogether, which involved careers advisers in working with groups, including, for example, the long-term unemployed, disaffected young people, or women returning to paid work.

It is clear, then, that in discussing 'group work' we are dealing with a range of activities and settings, and although there are common threads in terms of skills and processes and outcomes, definition is bound to be a primary issue. In fact, the different types of 'group work' a careers adviser may do from time to time can be plotted on a continuum from public speaking to interventions very close to individual interviewing. At one end will be formal presentations: these have their own rules and the skills required are fairly clear, whether the purpose is to 'sell' an idea or product, to present an argument for a plan of action, to inform a large number of people economically, or to report on the progress and outcomes of research or other activity. Voice projection, the preparation and delivery of visual aids, coherent, clearly structured arguments, and an effective way of dealing with difficult questions and objections are all part of the experienced practitioner's repertoire. There is little here which is specific to careers education and guidance.

Smaller group sizes (ranging from 'class size' down to about eight to ten people or fewer, and hence with much more opportunity for audience participation) are more typical of most careers advisers' interactions with groups these days. With the 'refocusing' agenda of the current government, another variant – 'group interviewing' with only four to five participants – is also making its appearance.[1]

The context is thus variable, and the careers advisers' own approach is fraught with uncertainty about role and purpose. While some advisers adopt the style of a 'subteacher', Higgins and Westergaard (1998) report that others go out of their way to avoid being identified with such authority figures and settle for making the occasion 'fun' at the expense of any measurable guidance outcomes. A third approach is a presentational style, delivering information about an occupation or a similar topic.

The best practice, as we shall try to argue in this chapter, involves none of these responses. The key reason for group work is the value of learning alongside, and partly from, other people: learning is a social activity and should take place in a social context. This has theoretical bases and practical implications. We propose to start with an exploration of what theory exists to provide a rationale for guidance in a group setting, and then develop ideas of how it might be realised in practice. We shall focus on interventions involving groups of 'class' size or less, whether in or out of an educational establishment, this being the usual context of delivery.

One purpose of theory is to make explicit the reasons why we do what we do. However, given the secondary role played by guidance group work in the past, by comparison with interviewing, it is no surprise to find that there is very little discussion of it in the extensive literature about 'group work'. Much of the writing on the subject focuses instead on therapeutic uses of groups, drawing on psychotherapy or developing sensitivity training or interactional skills. Other research addresses social case work or case management, for example in overcoming deviant behaviour, or deals with issues related to groups in community work and practice, or to deliver social training. Some of this can offer insights that could be translated with care into a careers education and guidance context, but generally does not offer much of practical value.

There are two key exceptions, one coming from a careers education perspective, the other from a careers guidance background. Bill Law (1996c) writes on 'Careers education in the curriculum' and prefaces this with an interesting distinction between careers education and careers guidance: though the boundaries between them are not always clear, the 'similarities . . . are as salient as the differences, so that skill and understanding in the one can often be used in the other [and] . . . a single programme of work can integrate them into a whole, each supplying mutually supporting contributions' (1996c: 210).

This endorses the practice of some traditional training courses for careers advisers in offering 'interaction studies' or some similar title to subsume both interviewing and group work and to emphasise the commonality between them. This also confirms that all careers work practice requires similar interpersonal skills, whether one is visiting an employer to find out about opportunities in the labour market, counselling a person at a crucial point in their career development, or interacting with a variety of groups of people seeking advice, guidance or support for work-related learning and development. Law goes on to develop useful distinctions between interventions that 'emphasise learning *generally* relevant to the group' using a *'ready made programme* articulated to what is known in advance to be useful' with 'movement *through the material* from "basic" to "advanced"' and 'acquisition of a general framework of learning (though capable of incorporating and supporting individual responses)' (1996c: 211, italics in original).

He associates these with careers education, and contrasts them with those approaches that are based on individual or small-group work using interpersonal processes emphasising 'learning *differentially* relevant to the individual . . . *negotiable*, not necessarily known in advance' with 'movement *through experience* towards what the client needs to do now [and with] readiness to deal with a *specific* problem or decision faced by one person now' (1996c: 211, italics in original). These he lists under 'careers guidance'. The two positions helpfully articulate a significant part of the continuum of group work above, from classroom sized groups to group interviewing and interviewing itself. As he says, 'this capacity concurrently to draw upon *group* processes, but to focus on *personal* experience, appears to be a key feature of successful group work' (1996c: 211, italics in original).

He later focuses briefly on methods and processes involved in the learning activities he subsumes under 'careers education', and he describes four broad types (1996c: 225–6):

- *Didactic*, where tight control is maintained by the teacher or the structure of the programme, and the participants have to attend to material that is presented to them.
- *Participative*, where learning is by doing, reflecting on active experience, discovering the learning points, working out how to do things, identifying and improving skills, learning to reapply them.
- *Experiential*, where learners' own ('value-laden') experience is central. As he describes it, 'there is no known-in-advance "right answer" to any issue': it is a matter of point of view. Such an approach is important where, as so often in careers education and guidance, the learner has to 'take a view' of what is being learnt, the material offered, and relate it to their own situation, attitudes, ideas and feelings. Law points out that this process is probably where individual guidance, group work and classroom-based careers education come closest to one another. The skills of 'neutral management' by the group leader, teacher or facilitator are very close to guidance skills as used in the individual interview. Conversation between participants is the important thing, with the facilitator acting like a good 'chair' of the meeting, 'an accurate and attentive listener – like a guidance worker'.
- *Experience-based methods*, where learning is by direct contact with people and real work or tasks in the community – as in work experience.

Law also draws a distinction between groups where communication is 'radial, arbitrated by a central authority' or 'orbital' in which participants help each other but keep in touch with the 'expert'.

It is less important, Law argues, to ask whether we should espouse the more traditional or the more progressive of these approaches, than to work out what to use for what purposes. He identifies three things that must be taken into account when answering this: (1) people learn in different ways, (2) variety is interesting, and (3) depth, breadth and progression require varied methods (1996c: 226).

Disappointingly, the focus of his analysis is not group work alone, but the larger context of careers education and its place in the curricula of the future. However, much of what he says about methods is highly pertinent. This is not surprising since group work is generally considered in the context of 'careers education', which, as Law defines it, is a much wider and more challenging concept than can be contained by a school or college curriculum alone, potentially occurring in all kinds of community interactions as citizens throughout their lives learn to play social roles in relation to each other.

Some of Law's themes and challenges are picked up by Higgins and Westergaard (1998: 39–47) in a paper entitled 'In search of guidance models for the group context'. Claiming that there is 'a lack of credible and theoretically based models for the delivery of guidance in the group context', they undertake a review of guidance and learning theories, and identify those that in their view form the basis for a 'unique model for the group context' (1998: 39). This paper is one of the few in the UK that directly attempts to provide us with a rationale for what we are doing in group work in this field. Higgins and Westergaard are both tutors at the College of Guidance Studies and experienced as careers advisers. They confirm from this vantage point some of the negative points we raised earlier in this chapter:

> despite the fact that group work is widespread, our experience . . . is that the potential of group work to achieve positive guidance outcomes . . . is not being realised in this country. Many guidance practitioners here seem to lack confidence in working with groups, uncomfortable in stepping beyond the presentation-style provision of specialist information. (1998: 40)[2]

They identify, as we noted earlier, the almost desperate attempts by some practitioners to avoid being labelled as 'teachers' and the corresponding insistence on making group work 'fun' and hence different from a 'lesson'. While this can trivialise the delivery of guidance outcomes in groups, Higgins and Westergaard believe that it 'derives primarily from the assumption that guidance skills can only be utilised in the one-to-one context, dealing with issues on an individual basis' (1998: 40). Consequently, guidance practitioners 'commonly label sessions "guidance" which are actually solely information-giving groups' where individual participants do not get the opportunity 'to reflect on their own position in relation to the topic' (1998: 40; cf. Law's description, above, of this as a key feature of both guidance and the experiential approach to careers education). This lack of clarity about the role of the guidance professional leads, they argue, to a reduction of confidence and credibility and hence effectiveness. They also point out that the traditional model of 'group talks' within a school-based careers education programme does not work in the great 'diversity of contexts within which practitioners operate'. Increasingly, group work occurs outside schools and colleges (and, now, with the disaffected and socially excluded, wherever they are or can be practically approached).

Their search takes them, first, through a review of models for individual interviewing, using Kidd's (1996b) classification. Various insights emerge from each. Thus the person–environment fit model would have little to offer since it would establish the role of the group leader as 'teacher and knowledge giver' and confirm the practices already criticised, whereas the person-centred orientation of Rogers would 'bridge the gap between "education" and "therapy"' (1996b: 44). They do not explain further. However, comparisons between the models of an individual interview and of a group work session can be fruitful.[3] It often helps trainees to understand the transferability of their skills from the one context to the other.

Most of the available interview models propose some common stages. There will almost certainly be an opening phase in which some sort of negotiation between participants and facilitator takes place. Even in a public presentation, it is good practice to share with the audience what you propose to talk about and why this has a bearing on their reasons for being there to listen to you. In less formal settings, as we move along the continuum towards the small group and one-to-one interactions, 'contracting' becomes more and more a matter of clarifying the purposes of the participants and identifying their needs – a crucial element of the effective interview, according to Bedford (1982). Any guidance intervention that did not manage to work out accurately what the needs of the participants were would be unlikely to achieve guidance outcomes except by accident. The creation of an appropriate rapport between audience and speaker, between interviewee and interviewer, between group leader and participants, is also a precondition most practitioners would recognise as part of good practice. Bedford (1982) emphasises this in his research finding that 'creating a friendly, encouraging atmosphere' is a necessary though not sufficient condition for an effective interview. Person-centred interviewers, too, accept such preconditions in stressing the importance of qualities such as genuineness, empathy and respect. At the other end of the interview or group session, most practitioners would acknowledge, in addition, the need for some summarising and a conclusion about next steps. Even the public speaker will usually attempt to round off their presentation with a reminder of key points and a review of key questions, if not actually proposing a list of actions to be taken as a result of his or her arguments.

There is therefore a considerable consensus on the broad model for guidance interventions, whether these are described as interviews or group work. There will be some effort at rapport building, setting an atmosphere conducive to whatever is to take place, and some effort at identifying the needs that are to be met by the intervention is also essential. At the other end of the process there will also be some attempt to summarise, pull together loose ends, and render coherent whatever issues or conclusions have emerged about the next steps to be taken or the implications for future behaviour. Such broad 'beginnings' and 'endings' are likely to be features of even the most informal interventions in outreach situations, though the 'ending' may be much postponed and the 'beginning' take place over a series of weeks or months while the practitioner establishes trust and confidence in the minds of those s/he hopes to work with.

It is in what happens between those two points that the greatest diversity will be apparent. How are the needs and issues elaborated? What activities, verbal inputs, questions or materials will be used to do this? How will participants be challenged, helped to learn, enabled to make decisions and so on? It is here that we need to draw down insights from other areas of theory to fill the picture in the frame.

Higgins and Westergaard (1998) rightly, in our view, turn to learning theory to answer this, since guidance is a form of learning and the outcomes of guidance as defined, for example, by the DOTS model (Law and Watts, 1977) are *learning* outcomes: self-awareness, opportunity awareness, decision learning and transition learning. One of the determinants of any practitioner's actions in a guidance intervention must be the outcomes identified as meeting the needs of the participants. As Law (1996c) said, in the passage quoted above, however, 'people learn in different ways' and this is one of the things it is necessary and particularly difficult to take into account when running a group as opposed to individual guidance. Kolb (1984) identifies four of these 'learning styles'. This is important not only because individuals differ, but because it represents the nature of learning, which, if fully accomplished, moves through a four-stage cycle, each stage of which may be more attractive to those with different types of learning style. The cycle begins with some actual experience (concrete experience) on which the learner then reflects (reflective observation), working out what happened, what it felt like, and so on. Some conclusions are then drawn and theories and generalisations are developed about the implications of those conclusions in other or similar contexts (abstract conceptualisation). Finally, it is necessary to test these theories out in the real world and see if they hold up in practice (active experimentation) to solve problems and make decisions. This, of course, then entails further concrete experience, and the cycle begins again.

As Higgins and Westergaard point out, experiential learning approaches derived from Kolb's theory (and, beyond him, from Lewin, Piaget and Crabbe) 'particularly complement the development of a guidance process for groups' (1998: 45). Since theirs is a theoretical article, they do not elaborate this further, but it is easy to see that the four-stage experiential learning model can both provide a space for the achievement of the DOTS learning outcomes (as they suggest) and accommodate our outlines for a group guidance intervention, provided we insert somewhere into the cycle an opportunity for a facilitator or interviewer to establish contact and agree a role for themselves in relation to the learner. There is a process going on here similar to that proposed for the interview. A phase of opening up the thinking and feelings of the participants is followed by summarising the conclusions, and agreeing on next steps, a plan of action to test out the new learning (see also Juch, 1983 for a summary and synthesis of 17 similar 'learning process cycles' and theories).

Kolb's cycle is proposed as a naturally occurring process, not one that only happens with the help of a teacher or facilitator. However, the experience which triggers it off can obviously be had in the classroom and be set up or arranged or designed by the teacher or facilitator. Role play exercises are an obvious example, but other group exercises of a more or less active or involving character – case studies, games, small-group discussions on an important issue etc. – can fill the space to some extent. The more lively and thought-provoking the experiences are, the better, since a more vivid and meaningful experience will be more memorable, and, from a guidance point of view, the more an individual feels themselves drawn into the activity and personally engaged and addressed by it, the more likely they are to be challenged 'to reflect on their own position in relation' to it (Law, 1996c). Designing/selecting and presenting such an opportunity for concrete experience would then be a central skill for the practitioner who wants to deliver an experiential learning group session. However, the group participants might already have had such an experience (for example, work experience or a visit to a local workplace) and the group session would then be about sharing it and the feelings and thoughts aroused by it and drawing out the learning points. So the cycle would begin at the reflective (what happened, what did you see, how did you feel about it?) or theoretical stages (so what does this mean for you, what conclusions can we draw from this?) and progress to the pragmatic, actively experimental (now what, how can we apply this, and in what new situations in the future?). Much of the value of role play will always be in the debriefing, and the same is largely true of any other activity or concrete experience, whether or not arranged/designed by the group facilitator. The raw data of experience must be transformed into personal meaning.

An important further claim is that individuals tend to feel more comfortable in different phases of the learning cycle. Thus some prefer to plunge into direct experience and sort out the learning implications afterwards. Such active learners will be happiest with project- and activity-based learning situations. Others, with a more theoretical learning style, might prefer to hear a full account of the rationale for the activity before taking part. Some will be impatient of any learning until it can be actively proven by experimentation, while others need to spend some time reflecting on what happened and how they feel about it, before committing themselves to any further experiments. The Learning Styles Inventory (Honey and Mumford, 1982; Kolb, 1985) elaborates this.

In any group session, then, there will be (1) a number of different learning style preferences among the participants, and (2) some attention paid to this by ensuring that the whole session addresses more than one of those styles. Ideally, all four should be catered for if the complete learning cycle is to be achieved. As Law (1996c) again observes, 'variety is interesting', but there is a more theoretical basis for it here: each person, to learn, needs an opportunity to do it their way. Activists in the group will learn best from some hands-on activity, theorists from drawing conclusions from that, reflectors from observing it and reflecting on what happened and how it felt, and pragmatists from the planning for active testing out of the learning points developed so that they can see its implications in practice. This underlines the value of small interactive groups with built-in feedback opportunities where the different needs of learners may be more easily catered for than in large assemblies and passive information giving.

The model for a small-group session, then, after the facilitator has introduced themselves to the group, established some rapport, and explained/agreed what is to happen and how this relates to their experiences and needs, would be:

1 Some relevant activity or hands-on exercise with participants probably working in subgroups of three or four.
2 A period of reflection on what happened and how it felt (was it difficult, easy, interesting, boring, what did you feel about it, etc.). This may be quite short, in some cases only a question or two from the facilitator or a few minutes within the small group to reflect or exchange thoughts and feelings with a partner; or quite long, where something like a role play has occurred that stirs up deeper emotions and requires significant debriefing to let the participants down gently and defuse any emotional difficulties. The phase may be split into two: individual reflection and whole group sharing or publishing of reactions and observations.
3 A phase in which the group, with more or less help from the facilitator or leader, tease out the learning points and summarise their conclusions from what they experienced. They may or may not reach consensus on this, but as far as possible all points of view should be respected and represented.
4 A final phase in which the loose ends are tied up, the conclusions summarised and the next steps clarified. This may be supported by additional reference materials or summary sheets for each participant to take away.

This is not intended as a rigid prescription, only as an illustration of how theory in this case can inform and, hopefully, inspire guidance practice. It avoids the dangers of trivialisation – what Higgins and Westergaard (1998) call 'making the session fun' at the expense of achieving real guidance outcomes – since that would involve skimping the last three stages for the sake of the first. It prevents the group leader or facilitator being seen as a teacher substitute, since it is about a negotiated *agenda*, not *curriculum*, and it disrupts the pattern of traditional 'information giving' which particularly disadvantages active learners and pragmatists alike. There are many active ways of presenting information (not just via the traditional and overused 'quiz') and, more importantly, of enabling it to be understood – to become personal knowledge actively incorporated by the learner.[4]

The experiential learning model obviously provides a rationale for what we do in guidance group work. It presents a practical design template for small-group sessions; it reminds us of the role of individual differences in learning style and that to learn properly is to do more than simply listen passively to what someone else says. It emphasises the role of the (participative) learner as opposed to that of the teacher, and that people are more likely to learn what they have discovered for themselves through experience than what has been simply presented to them. The idea of learning as development through a number of stages is also intuitively coherent with developmental approaches to careers education and guidance, and the notion that a complete learning cycle entails experience, reflection, generalisation and active experimentation, echoing career learning theory's phases of sensing, sifting, focusing and understanding (Law, 1996c).

Higgins and Westergaard (1998) also examine theories of student-centred learning (which offer a parallel to the client-centred approaches to CEG adopted by many guidance practitioners, and emphasise, as does guidance, key skills such as active listening) and andragogy. The underlying construct in both cases has as opposite poles the didactic and participatory approaches to learning/teaching, or as Knowles (1983; Knowles and Associates, 1984) has it, pedagogy versus andragogy. The latter is an approach designed particularly with adult learning in mind and is based on seeing the learner as self-directed rather than dependent (on the teacher or group leader); problem centred rather than subject centred (motivated to learn in part because of a desire to solve personally relevant problems and hence apply immediately what is learnt, rather than by the subject itself); bringing experience to the learning situation which must be taken into account as a resource; and ready to learn because of the demands of developmental roles.[5]

Though the model has been criticised, as Higgins and Westergaard point out, the caveats are as interesting for our purposes as the theory itself. Knowles amended his own position somewhat over time to suggest that pedagogy and andragogy were just two points on a continuum, alternative approaches to adult education and not the radically opposite poles of a construct, and that there were appropriate and inappropriate situations for using either method, depending on the target group, the content of their learning and the degree of relevant prior learning and experience they possessed. The contrast between adults and young people is also obviously taken as a metaphor for differential readiness rather than an absolute reality by Knowles's own followers, since several of the accounts of *Andragogy in Action* (Knowles and Associates, 1984) describe applications in schools and colleges with young people. As Law again reminds us: 'Depth, breadth and progression require varied methods' (1996c: 226).

What is at stake here is in part the role of the group leader, facilitator or teacher *vis-à-vis* that of the learner, student or group member. Guidance group work has in principle tended to side with student- and learner-centred approaches for the same reasons that it adopted similar theories to support person-centred models of individual interviewing as opposed to more old-fashioned 'test-and-tell' methods based on psychometrics. However, the questions raised by Higgins and Westergaard are important: what if the learner or client is not, after all, ready for such methods and needs more directive support? Even more telling in many of the practical contexts in which careers advisers have typically tried to do participative group work, what if the ethos of the educational establishment or the learners clashes with the assumptions of self-directed or participative learning? Careers advisers have often had only one session in which to deliver whatever was expected of them by the group or the school. They had little chance in such settings of building autonomous group learning if that had not already been achieved. So it is perhaps less surprising that many of them took the easy way out and settled for more passive forms that consorted with what group members and some schools and colleges expected.

The point is that the learning situation is very much determined by the learner's construction of it, and we ignore that at our peril. Constructivist theory has much to offer in this context. Piaget's contribution to the idea that the construction of knowledge is a dynamic process that requires the active engagement of the learner is probably one of the best known (e.g. Piaget, 1954). It clearly supports the kind of learner-centred process we have been describing. The personal construct theories of George Kelly (1955; 1991) are less commonly applied to CEG but are equally relevant.

One of the foundation statements of Kelly's theory is that unless you can anticipate the way others make sense of their experience, you cannot play a social role in relation to them. Role is a function of the way we anticipate how others make sense of ('construe') us. 'Role is an ongoing pattern of behaviour that follows from the person's understanding of how others who are associated with him [sic] in his task think' (Kelly, 1991: 68). Thus it is important that the guidance practitioner anticipates as far as possible the expectations the group have of his or her role in leading or facilitating them. If the group session is to be held in an establishment with a didactic and relatively authoritarian ethos, an attempt to carry out participative and experiential learner-centred group work may not be impossible but must expect to come up against some barriers, and the group worker may need to make his or her assumptions clear and explain in more detail the purpose and structure of the session. This may also be the case when dealing with some disaffected or socially excluded groups or those who come from some minority cultures: their experiences of group situations and of 'authority' figures may lead them to expect something different from the guidance practitioner. Not only so, but the invalidation of their expectations may, as Kelly defines it, produce anxiety – a state of mind consequent on finding that one's ideas about what to expect are of no use and do not make sense of what is happening (as, for example, on the first day at school or in a new job).

Clearly, then, it is important before running any group session to gather as much information about the group as possible, and, on meeting them, to spend as much time as is feasible finding out about their expectations of you and of the event. You also need to take account of their prior experience and understanding of the content of whatever process you have planned. If the session is to be about decision making, for example, what is their experience of decision making? Has anyone in the group made an important decision? Is it one they would be willing to talk about to others?

This raises a further issue where personal construct theory has some helpful insights to offer. One of the main reasons for giving guidance in a group rather than one to one is that group members (as Knowles and Associates, 1984 pointed out) have experiences and ideas to offer to each other and can learn from each other, in some cases, more than from the group leader. But if they are to do so, the atmosphere and ground rules, explicit or implicit, must be such that everyone feels safe in talking about matters that concern them and receiving feedback from the rest. It is the group leader/facilitator's responsibility to help create such an atmosphere, and this reminds us of Bedford's (1982) insistence on 'creating a friendly encouraging atmosphere' as a necessary condition of effective interviewing. In the group situation a further layer of meaning is added to this. According to personal construct theory both validation and invalidation, confirmation and disconfirmation, of one's constructs are a means of growth and development.[6] Other people are the prime sources of such validation and invalidation. We test out our ability to anticipate, particularly in situations involving other people. However, having a construct invalidated, that is to say finding that our hypothesis about the way someone else will behave is proved wrong, can be confusing, unpleasant or exciting, depending on a number of factors including the implications of that discovery for the rest of our construct system. In general, where group members are unfamiliar with each other and may share fewer common constructs about the group, its tasks and the content of any learning, it will be advisable to create opportunities for everyone to begin to make sense of each other and to anticipate the likely reactions to anything they may say or divulge. Omitting this will almost certainly mean that the group is less forthcoming, more cautious and unwilling to share important issues with each other. Putting pressure on them to open up, without first allowing time to make sense of the others and of you, is likely also to lead to more resistance or even hostility.

Both preparation and prior research on the part of the group leader, then, are clearly indispensable. So too is careful handling of the opening phase of the group session, giving the participants and the leader time to make sense of each other and to become comfortable with each other. Much of the success of such an occasion, as indeed with many interviews, depends on the framework in which it is set, both inside and outside the session.

So far we have emphasised the risks rather than the benefits. However, the group session offers its participants at best a means of growing and developing personally, a safe space in which to experiment with behaviour, to rehearse and try out points of view, before 'going live' in 'real life'. Kelly uses the metaphor of the 'personal scientist' testing hypotheses. Behaviour, he claims, is an experiment, and personality a form of movement. For the scientist, then, while invalidation of a hypothesis may be a setback in some ways, it does not need to be the end of the world. In the ideal group work situation one can take the risk of being proved wrong, because it is understood that taking such risks is OK and carries no devastating consequences, nor will it attract scorn or contempt from others. The group facilitator acts as referee and guardian of these ground rules, and will model the appropriate behaviour and attitudes by never putting down any contribution from a group member and by designing learning activities and situations that are insulated against serious invalidatory consequences for the people involved. Role play is perhaps the ultimate paradigm for this. As Van Ments (1994) points out in an excellent account, it can be used to do many things from describing or demonstrating a situation or problem, to demonstrating a technique or skill, practising that skill, reflecting on a situation or behaviour, or sensitising and increasing awareness of a situation or of others. The facilitator can control the degree of emotional feeling engendered in various ways, for example, by circumscribing the situation to be role played, or by putting the learner in the less vulnerable role and taking the hot seat him/herself. In personal construct terms, this involves limiting the area of the learner's own construct system that can be publicly invalidated, reducing the size of the wager the learner has to make that his or her hypothesis will turn out to be correct. It should not be overlooked that 'role play' does not have to be a fully 'staged' experience: being asked to briefly discuss or feed back on a case study 'in role' as one of the named participants ('Let's assume for a moment that you are the employer here: how do you feel about this interviewee?') is a form of role play, especially if another person or group is asked to respond to what has just been said, also in role. Case studies can also be particularly useful in this respect, since participants can discuss problems or decisions that are very like their own, without personally risking invalidation.

The key issue is to make invalidation, and hence reconstruction and development, possible without causing a participant to lose too heavily and hence retreat into what Kelly refers to as 'constriction' (a refusal to contemplate or make sense of the painful subject or issue) or 'hostility' (an insistence, in the teeth of the evidence, that a construct that has already clearly been invalidated still works).

Kelly's experience cycle has some distinct similarities with the experiential learning cycle, but describes in more detail how a person moves into and out of the process of active experimentation. As the group session begins, the participants will be in a state of *anticipation* in relation to what is to come: at least, one hopes to achieve this.[7] Then *commitment* or self-involvement takes over as the group facilitator explains and agrees with them what is to happen and how it is likely to relate to what they already know or have need of. They then become open to experimenting with new experiences. Next, there is an *encounter* with the learning event, where the experience is construed (perceived and made sense of) as fully as possible. As a result each person receives *confirmation or disconfirmation* of their constructs in the light of what happens and how they interpret it. In any case, there will be some kind of change, as the construct system undergoes *constructive revision*. (For a fuller account see Fransella and Dalton, 1990: 41–2.) Of course, all of this is achieved every time anyone experiences anything, but the group facilitator will try to ensure that the encounter is relevant, and properly prepared and planned. However, it should be noted that there may be several overlapping experience cycles taking place in the group, and not all of them will have to do with the explicit content of the session: for some participants the encounter with the facilitator or with other group members may be an experience cycle in itself and yield its own learning. One should cultivate appropriate modesty about one's importance on such occasions.

As well as the old adage, 'there is no such thing as teaching, there is only learning', it is perhaps useful at this point to recall Knowles and Associates' (1984) definition of an adult as 'one who has arrived at the self concept of being responsible for one's own life, of being self-directing'. They stress that in some learning situations even adults may 'be truly dependent on didactic instruction before they can take much initiative in their own learning; in such situations the pedagogical assumption of dependency is realistic' (1984: 12–13). Kelly also develops ideas about dependency. For him, however, the distinction between child and adult is not dependence versus independence, but the fact that a child is dependent on one person for most of their needs, whereas the adult has 'spread their dependencies' and in the event of need or difficulty can get help from a number of different people or places. This dependence is also reciprocal, not one-way: the adult recognises the need to give support as well as to take it (Maher, 1969: 189–206).

Translated into the group work context this helps us to make sense of the relationship between the facilitator/leader and the group members. As we have said, one key purpose of giving guidance in groups is to maximise the opportunities for learning from others as well as the leader, and this encourages spreading dependencies within the group. The reason for breaking a larger group into its smaller components, or getting people to discuss an issue with a partner, is not just to give the facilitator a break but to encourage the development of the group members and the group itself. On any topic there may be some in the group who can offer resources or help, and others who can get it from them, even if it is the sharing of a sense of how difficult or uncertain the task is; feeling 'I'm the only one here who doesn't understand this' can be a significant barrier to learning. Structuring the group session so that the learning points as far as possible come from within the group itself, by a process of discovery, might also be related back to the need to encourage people not just to rely on themselves, but to rely on the support and help of others to solve problems and understand issues – to wean them from dependence on the one 'expert' for all the answers.

Of course, this is an ideal scenario – many things can go on in small-group exercises and discussions that are not at all conducive to either positive learning or adult self-direction – but one goal of group facilitation will be to move in the direction of what Law (1996c) calls 'orbital communication'. This is when all the electricity no longer flows through the facilitator as an (overheated) junction box, but live connections are established between group members, who interact positively and seek support and validation from each other, not solely from the leader. If more than one session is available, this process of development can be more extensive and tangible. An effective group can be defined by the extent to which it achieves such reciprocally spread dependencies. As Johnson and Johnson (1987) observe, 'A group is two or more individuals in face-to-face interaction, each aware of his or her membership of the group, each aware of the others who belong to the group and each aware of their positive interdependence as they strive to achieve mutual goals.'

The future

There is no reason to suppose that groups will cease to be important in human learning. We almost all grow up in, and are sustained by, groups and communities of different kinds. They are the basis for our development, if you follow Kelly's (1991) reasoning, the source of vital validation and invalidation. In guidance terms, there is an additional reason for their importance: most of the outcomes of guidance tend to take us towards a work or employment situation in which we are likely to be testing out our constructs of ourselves and others in a work group of some kind. Learning to work in a team is supposed to be one of the key skills.

The future, however, will be heavily influenced as always by tech-nological developments, and 'groups' – social, supportive or work-related – are increasingly formed in cyberspace. Group work can operate in such a medium too, as many self-help, support and learning groups have shown. With or without a moderator, chat rooms, e-mail lists and newsgroups can offer new venues for our skills as guidance workers, though some of these may need some translation before they work in the new medium. Non-verbal cues may be absent, and often the guidance professional's credibility will have to rely on his or her writing skills. Asynchronicity also throws a new spanner into the works: what is the effect of having to wait 24 hours for a response to a question or to check out the meaning of an ambiguous statement, to hold such tensions in the mind over longer periods? Will different people come to the fore in using the new media in this way? There are as many advantages as well as disadvantages: the breakdown of barriers of social and geographical distance; nobody can see the traditional symbols of your superiority from your e-mails; and people who were previously isolated from guidance group sessions by disability or cultural factors may be able to take part on an equal footing at last. Role play in cyberspace, is, as we already know to our cost, even more realistically possible than in reality, but some people who would not have willingly tried it in physical space may find it a new form of active learning. So far, there have been only a few inconclusive experiments. They suggest, however, that the models and processes discussed here have a continuing relevance even in a technologically challenging future.

Far from being the poor relation of the one-to-one intervention, 'group work' is potentially a subtle, sophisticated and challenging process, with a clear rationale and distinctive skills, not just an inferior branch of teaching, a cheap substitute for interviewing or a quick way of delivering information. It is highly appropriate to the social and communal context of careers education and guidance.

Notes

1 It is quite controversial: some practitioners deny the possibility of 'guidance' being delivered in anything other than a one-to-one situation, and assert that the initiative is purely an economic contingency to sustain the fiction of a universal service in the face of cuts in resources. However, 'group interviewing' has been practised for at least 20 years in some services, and some regard it as a perfectly viable form of intervention, with an added diagnostic role: those who clearly need individual help can be identified in such a session, while others who would be over-served by such attention get what they need efficiently.

2 The distinction 'in this country' (that is, the UK) is perhaps a timely reminder that careers guidance practice in mainland Europe is often differently organised and that some of our concerns might prove to be a function of the historical division between a school-based 'careers teacher' and a 'careers adviser' external to the educational institution. The authors do not follow up this hint but it might be a useful starting point for further research.

3 By 'model' we mean essentially the anticipation any professional has of what is likely to happen in a given situation and what is likely to happen next, a series of phases or stages that an 'interview' or 'group session' may move through. Such anticipatory constructions are there to help the practitioner decide what are the appropriate activities, skills or resources to deploy and at what point, as well as forming a basis for the contract or negotiation with the client or clients. It does not predict or determine outcomes or content except at a very superordinate level. It is an extension of an everyday human need to anticipate what kind of event is about to happen in any given situation without, as far as possible, predetermining it or attempting to do so.

4 See also Jones and Pfeiffer (1980) for a more detailed treatment apart from careers work, and also at www.users.globalent.co.uk/~rogg/research/plerefs.htm where there is a helpful list of related references both practical and theoretical.

5 For an annotated bibliography of sources related to andragogy, including some critics, see Appendix A in Brockett and Hiemstra (1991).

6 A construct is technically a perception that two things are similar to each other in some way and different from a third. Thus one job might be seen as highly paid and another low paid, one person as friendly and another unfriendly. These would be two constructs: highly paid versus low paid, and friendly versus unfriendly. Typically a construct consists of a pair of such opposite terms or phrases or their unarticulated equivalents. Constructs represent the basic building blocks of our psychology: we use them to make sense of ourselves and others – rating ourselves as more highly paid but less friendly than another person, perhaps. Constructs are organised hierarchically in a personal map we use to anticipate future events, the likely behaviour of others etc. It may also be that one construct implies or subsumes another. Thus 'unfriendly' might for someone imply being highly paid, and they would then expect someone more highly paid than them to be less friendly to them.

7 Anticipation is the fundamental motivation in Kelly's psychology: we make sense of the world in order to anticipate future events and experiences, and how we do this channels and structures our personality.

5

THE DISCOURSE OF THE LABOUR MARKET

Why is labour market information important to careers education and guidance professionals?

The recent policy changes, leading eventually to the effective disappearance of the Careers Service as we have known it, raises, among other issues, the question as to what it is that marks 'careers advisers' out from other professionals in the field. Careers advisers are not social workers, youth workers, teachers or pastoral counsellors in schools, but the new Connexions service will include people from such backgrounds in the new and generic profession of 'personal adviser'. This is therefore a good time to point out that interpersonal skills such as those described in other chapters in this book are necessary but not sufficient for effective careers guidance. What makes that guidance distinctive is the application of, and reference to, expert knowledge and understanding of the labour market and its functioning. Careers guidance, in relation to counselling, we might argue, is an applied discipline in a way analogous to engineering's relationship to physics or maths. Both have their ultimate test in their effectiveness in creating and maintaining 'structures' that have to stand up and survive in a public world. If no one who received careers guidance could hold down a job or earn a living thereafter, there would be little basis for supporting it out of public funds, and, indeed, there might be a case for damages against practitioners of it for negligence. The newer term 'social inclusion' is but a wider and more flexible variation of this theme. The argument that guidance makes an effective and measurable contribution to the labour and learning opportunity markets is still essential to the political survival of the species.

Credibility with the public and with other professionals such as human resource development managers is also an issue. Traditionally, careers advisers working with the 14–19 age group visited a variety of workplaces on a regular basis, and prided themselves on the notion that they knew personally a large number of the local providers of employment and training. Until the trend towards staying in full-time education and training reduced the numbers seeking employment at 16 to below 10 per cent in most areas, the careers adviser not only helped his or her clients to decide what work they wanted to do but found most of them a vacancy with an appropriate employer and often arranged the interview personally. If the guidance given in the interview wasn't appropriate in the light of the 'real world' of work, if the needs hadn't been properly identified or sorted out and a viable action plan designed, the careers adviser could expect personal feedback further down the line. But those who seek guidance still do so because ultimately they want paid work and believe the careers adviser is knowledgeable about the labour market. Providers, meanwhile, continue to complain that guidance professionals do not understand enough about industry and commerce and do not spend enough time there to appreciate what is really going on.

The value of information to the guidance profession has always been clear. Despite attempts to separate them from guidance 'proper', informing and advising have always been important activities of guidance (UDACE, 1986). They do, however, draw on knowledge as much as skill. Information is the second outcome of guidance in FIRST, the five-outcome model of careers guidance proposed by Bedford (1982) and subsequently used as the basis for official inspections of careers advisers' interviews (though, as Bedford pointed out, the interview itself is not the most effective way of delivering it). More importantly, perhaps, 'realism' is the third outcome of guidance in FIRST: although controversial (no client-centred careers adviser would ever tell a client they were being 'unrealistic'), 'realism' is based on a close knowledge of opportunities and their structures and demands. Such knowledge prompts the careers adviser in the guidance conversation to ask certain questions so as to enable the client to discuss certain aspects of their experience, interests, abilities and values which could be relevant to the opportunities being considered. For example, if becoming a veterinary surgeon demands three high-grade A level passes in science subjects for entry, then a discussion of a client's own assessment of their potential at that level and in those subjects is a relevant topic, though it must be handled positively and sensitively. In the same way, if a client says they want to look after children, the adviser's knowledge of the types of work that could be involved informs the kind of issues they may suggest for discussion, and the areas of the client's experience they may feel it helpful to probe. Such approaches must, however, be informed by proper research and data sources, not by stereotypes or half-truths.

Feedback and advocacy are also included in the 'seven activities of guidance' (UDACE, 1986). To carry them out properly, guidance professionals need knowledge and in-depth understanding of how the labour market and education/training markets work, just as knowledge of how the law and the courts work is part of the expertise of the 'advocate'. To argue, for example, with an opportunity provider that a young person can cope with a particular type of work or course despite apparent unsuitability or disability, requires a more than cursory knowledge of what the work or the course, demands, what the employer or tutors expect of candidates and what arguments will likely persuade them. In some circumstances, for example where discrimination is possible, it may require a knowledge of the law as well. It is also envisaged that the guidance professional will influence provision by providing feedback to providers to encourage them, for example, to lay on new opportunities for groups hitherto overlooked or to adjust their approach to meet the needs of previously excluded populations. This, too, clearly requires knowledge of the market.

In various ways, therefore, relatively 'hard' knowledge of the external context in which career decisions are made is important to the 'internal' and interpersonal functions of guidance.

What is labour market information?

Labour market information (LMI) has been summarised as 'any information about the structure and working of a labour market and any factors likely to influence the structure and working of that market, including jobs available, people available to do those jobs, the mechanisms that match the two, changes in the external and internal business environments' (ADSET, 1995). That, of course, is a very wide ranging definition, which, if followed in detail, would leave the guidance professional with no time to do anything else. As Hirsh et al. (1998) report, the practitioners involved in their research 'were forceful in their view that different client groups may need different types of information and find different frameworks useful in their career decision making'. The age, life stage, qualification level, type of decision or transition, the guidance purpose for which the construct of work is to be used, and so on, all have to be taken into account. What then are the questions that guidance clients tend to ask, for which labour market data could contain the answers?

The following six areas were tested on a small sample of experienced careers advisers responsible for labour market information in different careers companies, and were generally agreed to be pretty comprehensive:

1 *Demand for labour* This involves questions such as, 'How easy is it to get a job in this occupation, industry or role?' and 'How competitive is it?' Answers have to do with matters described as skill shortages, replacement demand, expansion demand and the supply of labour. We might offer answers based on our knowledge of the number of vacancies compared with applicants pre- and post-training, whether it was a common or fairly common occupation or role as opposed to one with only rare or few vacancies, whether the occupation, industry or function is expanding or contracting, and whether the time a person tends to stay in the occupation or role is shorter or longer.

2 *Progression routes, career structure and earnings* The questions here will be of the type, 'What are the prospects?' and 'Where can I go from there?' To answer them, we would need to know something about initial and

later salaries, tenure or security level of the occupation or role, and its career structure – the opportunities for promotion and typical progression routes within it and to related opportunities. Some knowledge of further or advanced training programmes available, and of the extent of upward or sideways mobility, would be relevant.

3 *Geographical availability* The question here will mainly be of the type, 'How available is it in my (personal) travel-to-work area?' (Becoming a miner or lighthouse keeper, or even an air traffic controller, are jobs often limited by place.) But other questions may be implied, for example, 'How available is the training?', 'Where does it take place?' Answering these will mean knowing the geography of the area, and the routes and availability of transport (particularly important in rural areas). Knowledge of the wage rates offered – particularly if these are low – may be relevant (because of the need to pay for transport etc.), and sometimes also knowledge of the availability of accommodation, if the opportunities to work are outside the normal travel-to-work area.

4 *Trends* Is employment on the increase in this occupation or industry, is it stable, or are vacancies actually decreasing in the longer term? These are natural concerns for anyone investing in further learning, in particular, in preparation for a new career, or giving up a secure position in one industry to work in another. 'If I invest my time and money in getting trained, what are my chances of getting a job? How employable will I be at the end of the course?' The adviser will rely on previous research into destination statistics: where did graduates of this course go to in the past, how vulnerable to the economic cycle is this occupation or industry, have vacancies been notified to us increasingly or advertised regularly elsewhere, what signs have there been of the occupation/ industry expanding or contracting, what do we know about long-term versus short-term perspectives?

5 *Transferability* This follows on from the last set of questions, particularly if, as is often the case, the questions about future security cannot be answered satisfactorily. 'If employment in this occupation or industry or role should decrease markedly or die out, what else could I do with the training, the qualification, the competences and skills?' To answer this, the adviser needs to know how to elicit the competences, the breadth of the required base of skills in the present occupation, as well as where to find out about those in the area being considered or which might be considered. Some assessment of the general level of demand for the component skills will be relevant, too.

6 *Recruitment and selection methods* 'Where and how do people get jobs in this occupation?' Answers come from familiarity with the common routes into an occupation or industry or role, and with the processes employers adopt in recruiting and selecting for it – where vacancies are advertised, whether tests are used, and some idea of what employers are likely to be looking for from an applicant and how one traditionally applies.

Mapping the world of work

An adviser who mastered answers to all these questions would be an expert indeed, but in practice, of course, no careers adviser, even when experienced, is ever going to know more than 50 per cent of what s/he needs to answer questions about in day-to-day practice, and even less of what s/he might be asked on occasions. What is important is to know where to find the answers or, in the case of more knotty problems, where to begin the research, as well as a willingness to do that research if required or to make it feasible for the client to do the research for themselves, by defining what the questions really involve and where answers, if any, are likely to be found. This requires two things: a useful framework or set of templates to define the nature of the questions that are being asked, and knowledge of the whereabouts and layout of the data needed to answer them.

One task in the guidance interview is to elicit and explore the nature of the client's constructs of work and to help them set up experiments to test out their reliability and validity. These are their *personal constructs*. There are also sets of *public constructs* about occupations that make sense to a large number of us in a large number of contexts. They are *public maps of the world of work*. As guidance practitioners we need to know about them for three reasons.

First, they are used widely in official documents and reports on the labour and opportunity markets, and if we are going to use official data sources we need to be familiar with such constructs and their applicability to our clients' questions. Examples include the Standard Occupational Classification (SOC) scheme and the Standard Industrial Classification (SIC) system. These are official systems supported by the Office for National Statistics (ONS) and provide respectively a classification of occupations and of industries. For a fuller listing of both these systems see also *LMI Matters* (CTAD, 1996).

Second, they are used in classification schemes designed to help guidance clients and students in school, to structure careers libraries and so on. An example is the Careers Library Classification Index (CLCI) – a set of alphabetical codes that designate some occupations and functions as belonging to a group or family of jobs that may have some common interest for the guidance seeker. Its use is widespread in school and careers centre libraries and in occupational databases. It clearly aims to encourage a user to both focus on what is likely to interest them and increase the scope of their ideas within that and adjacent categories.

Third, they are used in psychometric assessments such as interest and personality tests. There are many psychometric classifications of characteristics relevant to performance and satisfaction in different types of work. They impinge on our mapping of the world of work, particularly through the increasing use of computer-based matching systems that try to describe the world of work in terms that can be used simultaneously to describe individuals and the roles and occupations available in the labour market.

Another approach starts from the essential set of skills exercised in a particular job or group of jobs or functions. This was one of the ideas behind the development of the National Vocational Qualification framework, now enshrined in the database of National Vocational Qualifications at the Qualifications and Curriculum Agency. In principle it is a categorisation of competence, but in defining the areas within which such competences are relevant, it implicitly maps the latter against the former, and may make it possible to see how individual skills can be transferred across occupational and industrial boundaries.

Constructs of work

There is currently some argument about the mapping of the world of work in terms of occupations. Occupation is traditionally defined (Watson, 1987) as 'engagement on a regular basis in a part or the whole of a range of work tasks which are identified under a particular heading or title both by those carrying out these tasks and by a wider public'. In this sense 'occupation' subsumes 'job'. An occupation is a collection of jobs. Job titles tend often to be specific to a company or a sector. Thus 'careers advisers' may be called careers officers, careers counsellors, guidance workers, careers consultants and so on, while carrying out what are recognisably the same or very similar sets of tasks: they form an occupation. However, employers in private industry often use job titles that have little to do with occupations as such and more to do with functions, roles or job level in the company – e.g. 'manager' (Hirsh et al., 1998). In addition, occupations may make the labour market look more static than it is and discourage change once a person has entered an occupation, whereas in practice people may move from one occupation to another more than once in the course of a working life. In the light of this, it is argued, more hybrid and multidimensional maps of the world of employment may be needed. Many careers services already use such a map based simply on the kinds of things clients ask about most often when presenting an information enquiry, rather than on academic research.

Even before we begin to tackle the market itself, then, there is difference, not to say dissent, over how we describe the basic building blocks. Whatever approach one adopts, however, the fact remains that in practice, by the time any client reaches a careers adviser, they are not a *tabula rasa*. There will be a number of personal constructs of work developed on the basis of a patchwork of influences, from family and social context, the media, and their own direct and often limited contact with work; and many of the influencers (e.g. parents, subject teachers, journalists and even some employers) will themselves have a limited understanding of the labour market, coloured by their own interests, values and experience. Much of the time, careers advisers' use of LMI will involve unpicking a client's ideas, correcting mistaken or narrow opinions, and offering alternatives to popular or conventional wisdom. This fits alongside the increasing need for labour market information lower down the school, as careers education moves into Years 7 and 8 and even into the primary school, and careers advisers are increasingly involved in the support for, and delivery of, curriculum materials.

To fulfil their role as those who know about the labour market, advisers must therefore understand some of the basic constructs of it and the often heated debates that take place over theories of its functioning. One must also understand the implications for guidance of taking sides in such debates. Otherwise controversial material will be presented as unproblematic, and the necessary interpretations of LMI offered to clients will simply reflect the most influential voice around.

A starting point is the classical economic view of the market. The market for labour is regarded as working exactly the same as the market for bananas. If we do not like what is happening in such a market, the reasons given will refer to an ideal model, the perfectly competitive market. Problems in such a market are, on this view, almost always the result of restrictions on the freedom of competition within it. There might be buyers or sellers who are acting as monopolists, big and strong enough, personally or through their organisations, to raise the price of the product by restricting the amount made or offered for sale. The products sold might be different, so that the preferences of buyers would be based on something other than price. There might be interventions by governments or other outsiders that distort the mechanism – by supporting the uncompetitive, perhaps, beyond the point at which they would have had to drop out of the market altogether. Buyers and sellers might not have comprehensive, accurate and up-to-date information about the opportunities to buy and sell, or there might be artificial and irrational restrictions on entry to or departure from the market, for example, in the labour market, by racial or gender discrimination. Mobility in looking for work may be inhibited by family or other considerations, which, though rational, are not purely economic.

The labour market obviously isn't perfectly competitive in several of these respects at all times and in all places. But many policy and legislative initiatives can be seen as attempting to make it more like the model: for example, by providing information to buyers and sellers through guidance agencies or job centres, taking action against discrimination that inhibits some sellers or buyers from joining the market on equal terms, and offering basic training programmes (literacy, numeracy, core skills and so on) so that individual sellers' labour is not inferior to that offered by more privileged groups.

Clearly guidance has a role, if a limited one, in such a model. For one thing, it can provide comprehensive, accurate and up-to-date information; it could try to challenge the rationality of discrimination on the grounds of race, gender or disability, thus increasing the freedom to enter the market on equal terms with others; and it might be able to help some people to be more mobile – leave the market, enter it, or move from one place to another to look for work – by information about sources of support for transitions, and problem-solving.

However, in the perfectly competitive market, supply and demand for labour would, on this model, be largely self-regulating. If more people want jobs than can get them, the price paid for their labour by the employer – the wage – will go down because supply of labour exceeds demand. If more jobs are available than people to do them – if demand for labour exceeds supply – the wages offered will tend to rise. The model is essentially about price plotted against available supplies. This is often represented as a curve on the two axes of a graph (Lipsey, 1989). If employers baulk at the current price of labour they may, for example, substitute machines for human labour, so the demand for labour will fall all along the curve, and at any given wage the demand will be less. Workers are in competition not just with other workers but with substitutes for labour generally as a 'factor of production' – something employers can use to produce the goods they want to produce. There have been vivid accounts, over the last 20 years, often exaggerated, of the way technology threatens to substitute for labour (for example Rifkin, 1996).

In the perfectly competitive model there is an equilibrium point where supply and demand match each other, and the market stabilises. This homeostatic mechanism is the desired end of labour market policy based purely on such a theory. The goal is the equilibrium market price of labour: the wage at which supply of labour, and demand for it, are equal, and thus the market 'clears' with no long-term skill shortages or involuntary unemployment (Adnett, 1989). Not only does this explain the labour market, it explains unemployment – which, on this showing, would be due to restrictions on the price or supply of labour, by union bargaining or restrictive practices, by government intervention or regulation, and by unrealistic wage demands by the workforce.

The argument about whether the actual labour market should be seen as simply an aberration from the pure competitive free markets of classical and neo-classical economics underlay the government policies of the UK during the 1980s and early 1990s. Government's role, according to this view, is to ensure that the institutions of society – unions, professional bodies, the family etc. – are unlikely to interfere with the 'natural' workings of the market. It may do this, for example, by providing childcare facilities to enable women with young children to return to paid work, by legislating to reduce the power of trade unions, by deregulating entry to professions, and by abolishing institutions such as the Wages Councils, which interfere with the process by setting a minimum wage for certain occupations.

If you accept this explanation of the labour market you will probably see guidance principally as a lubricant, intended to ensure the smooth functioning of the mechanisms of the market – for example, by providing accurate and up-to-date information to the buyers and sellers in the market, and by ensuring everyone has the necessary job search skills and a 'realistic' attitude to wages. Guidance is there to remove obstacles presented by individual behaviour which interfere with the smooth matching of individuals and vacancies.

But markets are rarely 'perfect', least of all labour markets. Nor is this simply a matter of the odd imperfection: even within economics itself, segmentation theory has challenged the classical model. There may be not one labour market but many: for example, competition for jobs at one level of entry qualification or in one geographical area may be relatively independent of competition for jobs at a different level or in a different area. This makes good sense in practical experience. The market for doctors is clearly not the same labour market as the market for cleaning staff or nannies or salespeople, and what happens in one of these markets may not affect what happens in the others at all. Despite the assumed impact of 'globalisation', the market for labour in north-east England may function very differently from that in southern England.

In the simpler versions of segmentation theory, dual labour markets can exist even within the same company, with a primary labour market comprising all those jobs with good working conditions, high wages, job security, promotion prospects, good on-the-job training and a well-ordered internal labour market in a particular firm or occupation. In such a labour market, entry to jobs is on the basis of skills and educational or professional attainment, and access to higher-level jobs is via an internal career structure. External mobility – people moving out of or into the market is going to be low except at the highest occupational levels. If you cannot gain entry you are restricted to secondary sector jobs.

This secondary sector offers jobs with low pay, poor conditions, insecurity, few prospects and little training. Jobs here will be filled largely by recruitment from the external labour market. There's a lot of mobility between jobs and occupations but not much progress up or down: the workers remain at the same relatively unskilled level. If you're disadvantaged by not having exam passes or the right social background you'll be most likely to end up in the secondary sector. The high turnover rate in the secondary sector can be a disqualifier for those who want to move into the primary labour market, as employers there tend to see such an employment record as a sign of an employee's unreliability. So working in this sector can be a self-perpetuating disadvantage. At its fringes the secondary labour market has seasonal workers and those on low-security short contracts, illegal immigrants, sweatshops, informal 'black economy' work and so on. It may also be more common in some inner city areas. Racism and sexism may be involved in its creation in some circumstances, too.

There are clear implications for guidance. To get into the primary labour market you need training and encouragement to forgo jam today (the prospect of an immediate job) for the possibility of jam tomorrow (the prospect of a better and more secure job later). This means getting in early and telling students in school what the reality is like out there, making plain to them the consequences of certain choices. It may be that some young people will be condemning themselves to a life of insecurity and low earnings which is self-perpetuating. This is also an approach that fits with the current Labour government's attitude to the role of the Careers Service, which requires them to work hard to increase the numbers of young people in learning as opposed to work in the 16–19 age group. The implication is that more learning will mean less time later on benefits or welfare – a feature of the primary rather than secondary labour markets.

On this view, also, careers advisers have a responsibility to advocate the cause of those they advise and help who are disadvantaged by the labour market through no fault of their own. Racism and sexism need to be challenged intelligently, with recognition of the often unconscious discrim- ination that occurs through restriction of access to primary labour markets. People with disabilities may also suffer in this way. Careers services need to feed information back to the appropriate organisations in training, employment, education and government, and to support and encourage the development of training programmes that help to overcome the barriers suffered by disadvantaged groups. This is as much because this situation (unlike the ideal purely competitive market) is not rationally constructed: it leads to employers and the country generally being deprived of competent workers and a pool of potential skills remaining unused.

A further consideration is that much of the careers literature in careers libraries and a majority of the careers discussed with young people appear to describe work in the primary labour market. Yet, on this theory, large numbers of people – increasing in the future – may in fact work in secondary labour markets. Some people (including people in developing countries) will have to work in secondary labour markets whether they like it or not, short of a revolution in the world economy. It might be argued that careers advice adapted to the needs of such workers has not yet been properly developed: we could do much more to improve the advice we give to such people with a view to helping them to survive in such markets. This might be more detailed advice about employment rights, relevant trade unions, welfare benefits, in-work benefits, funding for training, average wage levels, voluntary work, coping with unemployment and so on.

As Rubery and Wilkinson (1994) point out, however, it is nearly as hard to find evidence of purely segmented markets as it is of perfectly competitive ones. Segmentation is more complex, and the supply side of the equation is as likely to be segmented as the demand. Firms' own policy and strategy have a considerable impact on local labour markets, both internal and external. They argue that in fact it is necessary to go right down to organisational level to understand 'the dynamics of change in the employment system . . . This is in contrast to the market approach of the neo-classical economist' but at the same time requires an understanding of 'the influences of external conditions on internal employment practice' (1994: 66).

Although simplistic in itself, the segmentation model and its accom- panying critique are nevertheless closer to the messy reality we confront as careers advisers than the classical economic model. The economic relationship between buyer and seller of labour is affected by other than economic factors – group norms, social interactions, the influence of 'institutions' (professional bodies and trade unions, for example, or the worker's family). Neither the individual nor the firm has time to gather the complete information necessary for perfectly rational decisions about job seeking or employing people. It is always a compromise. Firms may be able to operate successfully in one way in one context, but the same strategies will not work in another. These strategies, however, 'create for each individual employer the labour market environments, internal and external to the firm, which act as important constraints on the range of employment strategies that an individual employer can devise and deploy'.

Relations of production are social as well as technical and the functions of the former, as Rubery and Wilkinson (1994) point out, are coordination (getting people to work together) and control (exercising power and imposing sanctions). A major difference between the market for carrots or TV sets and that for labour is that, in the latter, buyers (employers) do not own what they buy: they buy the worker's willingness and ability to work, but there is scope for conflict and competition in extracting the optimum out of the situation for either side. This is one rationale for paying higher wages, not just the scarcity of labour. There are local and specific asymmetries of power in this process, and not all on one side: 'for example, capital's economic superiority and control of the means of production [ownership of the factory, the machinery, the funds] is countered to varying degrees by trade union organisation, skill scarcity, and the privileged access labour has to information about production processes acquired by work experience and . . . learning-by-doing' (1994: 29). If either side withdraws cooperation, it may inflict losses on the other that cancel out the gains. Sacking experienced workers because they cost too much will also cost you money to recruit equally skilled ones or to train them to the level of the others. Compromise is not just about job seeking, but also about the level, type and rate of work once you are employed.

As Peck observes:

> The local labour market is more than a deviation from some national average (itself, obviously, only the sum of local conditions within a national space); instead it should be understood as a territorially constituted social structure. (1996: 266)

People are not as mobile as goods. They will not necessarily move to wherever their skills are needed (they have homes, relationships, family and friendships, roles in the community). When the coal mines are shut down, where do the miners go? Do they go there at once? What difficulties do they face in doing so? Nor are skills necessarily fully transferable: they may have different values in relation to different job opportunities

Why does it matter to a careers adviser? There is a clear alternative here to the view of guidance as a lubricant of the free labour market. Social and political factors have to be taken into account as well, and guidance can arguably be seen to have a role in relation to them, and not just at an individual level either. Guidance workers are involved with individuals in the front line and that is their starting point, but they may, on this analysis, have a role to play in representing their clients' interests and influencing social and political structures on their behalf, or, more progressively, in empowering and enabling their clients to influence these structures for themselves (cf. UDACE, 1986).

Sociological views of the labour market, then, try to explain labour markets in terms of social groups, relations and institutions. The need that human beings have to exchange goods and services leads to the formation of new social groups: employers, workers, firms, occupational groups, trade unions and so on. There are also new social relations – e.g. between capital (those who invest in industrial and other activity), management and labour, and new social systems such as employment, systematic training or industrial relations (Fevre, 1992). Careers guidance services can be seen, in this theory, as one of the institutions that have grown up around the labour markets in some countries.

Institutions such as these influence the structure and functioning of the labour market. All of these may lead to restrictions on or regulation of (depending on your viewpoint) the 'pure' freedom of the market. Systems of training and industrial relations are set up. People and groups gain vested interests in furthering the gains of their group as a whole, as a means to ensure security and other benefits for themselves as individuals. The motivations here are more than simply economic, if by that we mean a concern with the price of, and reward for, labour.

The family, too, in a different way, acts as an 'institution' within the labour market. Households make economic decisions, not just individuals, and implicit or explicit 'deals' are made within them about who is to do the paid or unpaid work involved in maintaining a family. These have longer-term sociological implications, such as an improvement or a deterioration in the social position of either gender within the labour market. Families also play a role in producing or reproducing orientations to paid employment, especially in terms of what is regarded as 'suitable' for one gender or the other. Such attitudes are seldom held on purely economic grounds. The demands of partners, childcare and eldercare often affect women very differently from men. There are many hours of unpaid work involved in 'reproducing' the labour force – feeding, resting, reassuring, training and socialising it to operate effectively as the employers or other organisations of the labour market require (Watson, 1987: 212–13). The 'labour supply' that is paid for at the point of exchange in the market is the product of investment of a lot of time and effort for little or no direct financial reward by many other people apart from teachers and trainers. When it is no longer needed, it also has to be looked after at least minimally, lest the current workforce become demoralised by the prospect of what is to come.

One advantage of sociological approaches is that they offer a much more serious attempt to deal with discrimination and disadvantage in the labour market than purely economic ones. Economics can tell us that race discrimination is irrational: even classical economics does not support it. All should have equal access to the market, and the free movement of migrants is another necessary condition for perfect competition. Explaining irrationality, however, requires us to go outside economics itself; the reasons people are disadvantaged in the labour market are inextricably linked with social and political explanations. Careers guidance, because its achievements are ultimately validated or invalidated on any theory in the context of the labour market, is also inevitably involved in issues of advantage and disadvantage, rationality and irrationality, and hence social and even political activity

Future work: a changing labour market?

One of the important variations of segmentation theory is Atkinson's (1985) model of internal labour markets in the 'flexible firm'. This transposes the primary/secondary divisions into core versus periphery, with secondary labour market employees split into full-time but relatively insecure employees and those on even less secure part-time or temporary contracts, while certain specialist work is outsourced entirely. Flexibility may be either functional – the same worker is multiskilled – or numerical – the numbers employed may be increased or decreased without much difficulty. Handy (1989) also popularises the idea using the image of the shamrock to stand for a three-leaved labour market with a core of professionals, technicians and managers, a fringe of self-employed or subcontracting specialists, and the flexible labour force of temporary and part-time workers, claimed to be the faster growing group. In part this notion falls to the criticisms already detailed in Rubery and Wilkinson (1994), but its ideas about employers' approaches to flexibility signal the establishment of a view of the labour market which has come to be not only dominant in the literature about careers education and guidance but accepted as uncontroversial. Not just the organisation but the labour market is moving in the direction of increasingly insecure and flexible employment. Thus Bayliss (1998) declares: 'People are becoming used to change; the idea that there are no more jobs for life goes largely unchallenged . . . the concept of a public sector career, or a business career or a career in a single occupation, has gone.' This is so certain that the Royal Society of Arts report in question offers no references to any evidence, as if it were indeed a consensus beyond dispute by all right minded people. The supporting argument may be briefly summarised as follows.

In 20 years the world of work will look very different. There will be few fixed boundaries between sectors and businesses, or private and public sectors. All boundaries are fluid and change often. The notion of a career in a single occupation will have largely disappeared. Growth of part-time and short contract work will be significant. Individuals will move frequently between different kinds of employing organisation. Most people will be working but in roles not jobs, achieving outputs not tasks. People will work where their skills can be used. The needs of employers, wherever and whatever they are, are much the same. Employability (the result of high-quality training) replaces job security. 'Knowledge work' is the most important thing. Lifelong learning to cope with frequent changes will be required, too. Core skills or key skills are what is required, not job specific skills. More and more organisations will be 'virtual' without a specific geographic location. Work will be a matter of outputs contracted to individuals, not something demanding attendance at a fixed place for fixed times. Employers will act as customers. The employed will adopt self-employed attitudes. Pay will be performance related. Environmental pressures and the impact of information technology are key factors and firms will seek to achieve cost reduction. There will therefore be more teleworking.

There are clearly significant implications for guidance practice. Guidance will be required throughout life, rather than just at the entry to the labour market, but in return has to rethink what its purpose is when apparently stable 'careers' are no longer available, so that any choice is just a brief turning point in a story that contains many of them. It is not surprising that narrative versions of career theory have developed in parallel with this view of the labour market. When the future is so insecure and uncertain, the function of guidance may be to enable individuals to make personal meaning out of the relatively chaotic events that make up their lives. *Positioning for the Unknown* was the title of one report on career development for professionals in the 1990s (Watkins and Drury, 1994). The 'importance of the subjective career: that is, the sense that individuals make of their careers, their personal histories, and the skills, attitudes and beliefs that they have acquired' is that 'it is more up to individuals to clarify their own values and to define what career success means to them personally' (Arnold and Jackson, 1997: 429).

There are clearly arguments for the trend to a flexible labour market which offer more in the way of data to support it – for example Rajan et al. (1997). However, they are much more cautiously worded, as you would expect from an empirical study. For example: 'this new form of flexibility is much more evident in fast growing service industries; elsewhere not much research has been done . . . the shift towards greater flexibility has, however, been challenged on the basis of certain official studies; the figures used, however, are somewhat outdated' (1997: 43). There are also a number of attacks on the simplistic versions of the argument, from different quarters. The TUC report *The Future of Work* (2000) summarises a number of official studies up to 1999 and concludes that the death of the permanent job is very much over-hyped: 'What official statistics show is that the permanent employee remains the bedrock of the UK labour market.' They quote the Labour Force Survey to show that while permanent employees were

82.8 per cent of all in work in 1984, the percentage had dropped to 81.7 per cent in 1999. This is hardly a 'careerquake' (Watts, 1996d). They also note that 'people stay in jobs almost as long as they did fifteen years ago. The share of long tenure jobs in the economy appears to have changed remarkably little.' Coming from the TUC one might expect little enthusiasm for the idea of a flexible future, but they simply confirm what academic researchers with less clearly political positions have argued. Rubery and Wilkinson (1994) concluded that: 'There is little general evidence that employers have systematically pursued such objectives as greater labour force flexibility, de-skilling, human resource management, or have adopted the "new industrial relations".'

This debate is likely to continue. What is important is less who 'wins' the 'Fordist/post-Fordist, flexible/permanent, local/global' debate than the reasons why it is argued in the first place and the fact that it is still hotly contested. In the most recent account of the arguments, Bradley et al. (2000) speak of 'the increasing tendency for the study of work relationships to be framed by concepts employed by managers (such as flexibility, empowerment, performance management)'. They claim that 'Our argument is not so much that "myths" are deliberately used to mask reality, as that particular versions of reality have more power to "stick" than others and so become popularly accepted.' They then proceed to carefully deconstruct these – globalisation, lean production, non-standard employment, the skills revolution.

The question that guidance professionals should be asking themselves is why such 'myths' are apparently so sticky and have been so sensationalised in the careers education and guidance community. Brown points out that when working with people displaced or dislocated by real changes at work, the scenario will be attractive because it seems 'to offer the possibility of an individual rebuilding her or his career on different lines' and clearly one wants to avoid the danger, as a guidance professional, that in such circumstances they will 'lock themselves into defensive or regressive choices (for example, searching only for jobs directly comparable to the ones they have just lost) rather than career choices that are developmental and progressive' (1997: 2). He argues, however, that 'polemics about changes to some middle class careers, serve to misdirect attention away from aspects of the changing patterns of careers which should be of more pressing concern to guidance practitioners: most notably the effect of an increasing bifurcation in the labour market between jobs requiring relatively high and relatively low levels of skills' (1997: 3).

What is a matter of concern is the way the 'polemic' Brown describes regularly surfaces now even in careers education materials. In a new *Work Skills Resource Pack*, for example, Helen Vandevelde (2000) (described in the foreword as 'combining the talents of Charles Handy and Ruby Was, with a gift for anticipating trends in the workplace'), after acknowledging that the rhetoric about the end of work 'bit the dust' at the 'dawn of the millennium', goes on to repeat the same mantra:

We change jobs more frequently than we used to. We combine work with study, often from a very early age. Some take a year off work to go backpacking or defend the countryside against motorway contractors. The numbers of self-employed have been rising fast and those with short term contracts and in part-time work have soared, with many juggling several contracts simultaneously.

The materials offered in the pack address related themes including 'new age working'.

The arguments are no longer presented in such a context as arguments: they are facts of nature, which young people and other clients of careers education and guidance are positively discouraged from questioning. Flexibility, moreover, is not just inevitable, it is good for you. But this too, is contested. Sennet (1998) offers an alternative picture of its impact on personal character. There is no part of this discourse, in other words, which is not under challenge. Such a debate is healthy and educational – a worthwhile part of a careers education programme, even.

The present situation is at least as much due to the intervention of governments, for example, as to faceless global forces: the 1980s in Britain saw a major shift of power from workers and their unions to employers, and a serious deregulation of the labour market, as well as major privatisations of public organisations including careers services. This broadly continued in the 1990s. If manufacturing declines, governments can either try to halt that decline or ignore it. At a global level, international organisation and agreement can bring about financial stability, as it did in fact until the 1970s. We are at the mercy not of inanimate forces, but of other human beings and social institutions.

The practice of careers guidance is inevitably political, in the sense that the labour market is a place where power is exercised and governments and other social institutions have interests they actively pursue there. Changing governments often bring changing guidance practices, as we know from recent experience in the UK. This view is also reflexive: careers guidance is a social institution, a player alongside others, with its professional interests and concerns for status and influence in society.

The guidance community has to accept that it too is part of the situation, not a neutral observer somehow above the fray and offering advice from afar. If it decides to take a certain view of the labour market and its functioning as read, that will influence the way careers advisers and careers teachers operate, the ends they pursue and the policies and strategies they develop to do so. The prophet is part of the prophecy. In economics above all, we know that a few words by people in high places can bring about national, even global consequences. This is perhaps one more of the things that render the labour market unlike the market for bananas or TVs: if enough people say there is going to be a recession and convince enough other people they have a point, there may well be a recession even if it was unlikely otherwise. In the same way, if enough people say the future is flexible, that we shall change occupations eight times in our lives, and become self-employed portfolio workers on short contracts, with small cores of highly paid and overworked employees ring-fenced against the dire insecurity (and poverty) of the rest of us, such a scenario may come a step closer. If people look to careers advisers and guidance professionals as experts on the subject, it is up to us to be careful what we say: careless talk costs lives in more senses than the original one.

6

CAREERS EDUCATION

A planned programme of careers education and guidance is an essential part of the curriculum, since it encourages young people to prepare for their future lives. But work and careers are not what they were. The changes brought about by technology and new working practices mean that people need to be more flexible, willing to continue to learn and able to plan and manage their careers.

Sir Ron Dearing, Foreword to *Looking Forward* (SCAA, 1995)

The context

Careers education and guidance have occupied an important place in the changing policy agenda for education in the UK during the last 20 years. In that time, great strides have been made in the provision and resourcing of careers education and guidance supported by committed staff in schools, colleges, universities and careers services. Careers education and guidance have attained a high profile in contemporary curriculum debates, championed by governments, by business organisations, and by schools, colleges and community organisations. At the level of policy, careers education has moved from a marginal position at the periphery of the curriculum to occupy a position centre stage in many schools and colleges. This is particularly evident with guidance processes in the curriculum, which currently form an essential component in raising achievement strategies associated with the teacher-led activities of student academic review, target setting and performance measurement. Information, advice and guidance are now becoming a central part of the role of many teachers, lecturers and community mentors.

The mantra of careers education and guidance has formed a core element in many contemporary educational initiatives targeted at the Key Stage 4 and post-16 curriculum. Careers education and guidance are incorporated to help address many of the challenges to the lives and experiences faced by young people when progressing through the transition points and pathways encountered through the education system, and upon entering the labour market. The place of careers education and guidance in the curriculum has therefore moved from being primarily concerned with helping students to obtain information and to choose a job on leaving school, to become an integral part of the political and economic policy landscape for raising achievement, social inclusion, economic competitiveness and lifelong learning.

On the ground, however, the experience of careers education and guidance for many students continues to be variable between educational institutions, and between geographical locations. Careers education and guidance retain a tenuous foothold in the curriculum of many schools and colleges, and are excessively reliant upon the continuing support of senior managers, and the goodwill, enthusiasm, energy and dedication of careers coordinators and careers advisers. As a consequence, repeated surveys of the practice of careers education and guidance in schools and colleges indicate huge variations in the quality of provision, and highlight the vulnerability of careers work to the whim of changes in policy direction by governments or by schools or college managers (see surveys by NACGT, 1989; 1999; NACGT/ICG, 1993; 1996; OFSTED, 1995, 1998a).

This chapter contextualises the development of careers education and guidance practice in the curriculum of schools and colleges in England. The chapter starts by revisiting definitions of the terms 'career' and 'careers education'. This is followed by a contextual historical analysis of the evolving place of careers education in UK educational policy, and as an aspect of the school and college curriculum. This critical analysis considers the current structural strengths and weaknesses of the place of careers education and guidance in the curriculum, and draws upon sources of evidence contained in the literature as well as the personal reflections of careers coordinators, careers advisers and students. The final part of the chapter will attempt to map a way forward for careers education and guidance within the context of the emerging 14–19 curriculum framework and the Connexions strategy (DfEE, 2000a). An attempt will be made to identify current areas of opportunity and issues facing the development of careers work, and to tentatively provide examples for the practical development of careers education and guidance in schools and colleges in the new context.

The key points contained within this chapter are:

- Careers education and guidance are essential for all students, and should be an integral, recognisable and progressive aspect of the curriculum starting from early years education and continuing into post-compulsory education, training and employment.
- The current place of careers education and guidance in schools, colleges and the universities can only be properly understood in relation to an analysis of the evolving social, cultural, political, educational and economic context.
- The concepts underpinning our understanding of the rationales for careers education and careers guidance are ambiguous, 'contested' and

subject to repeated redefinition in order to make careers work fit the prevailing policy concerns. As a consequence, the practical reality of careers education and guidance programmes in many schools reflects the lack of coherent philosophy and ambiguity of purpose.

- The dominant driving policy strategy behind the growth of careers education and guidance as a policy imperative over the last 20 years has been to meet the skill needs of economic competitiveness and global competition. It will be argued that this policy rationale is too narrow to sustain careers education and guidance in future curricula, and that an urgent redefinition of the operational rationales for careers provision needs to take place in order to help address fundamental issues of social justice.

- Whilst there have been significant developments and improvements in careers work during the past 20 years, it remains a neglected and peripheral curriculum activity in many schools and colleges.

- Careers research and theory are often perceived to be 'out of touch' with the everyday concerns of practitioners in the classroom, and there is little evidence of understanding of how career theory can inform practice in most schools and colleges. There is therefore an urgent need for research and theory to be rearticulated and presented in ways that provide curriculum managers and coordinators with a coherent and practical basis for action.

- Careers education and guidance in schools and colleges needs to be re-energised and reconnected with the real need of individual students and their communities. It is essential that curriculum planners establish mechanisms to actively engage students, their parents/carers, and local communities in designing and delivering provision that is relevant to their needs.

- The current context for the 14–19 curriculum provides opportunities for a review of careers curriculum provision in schools and colleges. In Key Stages 1–4, there is a need for practitioners to redesign careers provision as a component of an integrated personal, social, career health, citizenship and work-related curriculum, underpinned by tutor-based planning and review guidance processes.

- The emergence of the Connexions strategy and the revised National Curriculum present new and exciting opportunities for the development of an integrated and student-led approach to careers education and guidance.

What is 'career'?

The chapter begins with a discussion of the changing concept of 'career'. Watts (1983; 1999) argues that to understand what is meant by careers education and guidance, it is necessary to understand that the term 'career' has changed, for which the evolving context was described in some detail in Chapter 1. Watts argues that the concept of 'career' is a derivation of the 'late industrial era' associated with the breakdown of 'traditional mechanisms of role allocation within social classes [that] ceased to be sufficient to cope with the pace of economic and industrial change' (1999: 1). The 'traditional' conception of career is exclusively middle class, 'concerned with progression up an ordered hierarchy within an organisation or profession' (1999: 1). This 'bureaucratic' conceptualisation of career (Collin, 1996) has become associated with a view of organisations as hierarchical, dominated by specialisation and internal labour markets providing corporate ladders for individuals to climb. However, this traditional view of organisational and occupational structures does not bear close examination for the majority of citizens. As Collin (1996) points out, the 'careerless' majority have always had jobs that fall outside this organisational model, often in short-term, insecure, poorly trained and ill rewarded 'jobs', or as part of the huge number of unpaid homeworkers, unemployed, or workers in the informal economy. Hence the comment, 'the middle classes have careers, the rest of us just have jobs!'

As Chapter 1 demonstrated, this bureaucratic model of organisations is now becoming outdated, rendering the traditional conceptualisation of career as outmoded. The new 'career realities' (Kidd, 1996a) are that responsibility for career management is increasingly with the individual, with major implications for the development of learning career skills and attitudes. The rhetoric of personal responsibility formed a central theme in the political ideology of successive Conservative governments of the 1980s and 1990s, and has been appropriated by the New Labour government through the lifelong learning and skills agendas (Edwards et al., 1998). 'Objective' career paths are being replaced by 'subjective' careers which emphasise self-direction and personal autonomy' (Kidd, 1996a: 142). Watts (1999) agrees that the bureaucratic model of 'careers' in organisations is fragmenting as entry and progression points become less secure, and as traditional linear career pathways disappear, 'disturbing the dialectical relationship between the individual and the organisation' (Collin, 1996). There is no doubt that the process of post-industrialisation has created problems for career theorists and policy makers concerned with careers education and guidance, necessitating a critical rethinking and reconstruction of the concept of career. Savickas suggests that 'career theory is at a crossroads' (1994: 19), and is being problematised in a postmodern world that has 'de-mythologised, de-legitimated and de-constructed it' (1994: 20).

Much current theory emphasises the inclusive nature of career rather than the previous external and hierarchical construction outlined above. Social constructionists emphasise the personal, subjective, interpersonal and community construction of career, rather than 'career' as an objective reality. As Collin suggests, career is concerned with the 'unfolding interaction between a person and society over time. It has several faces: individual and society, objective and subjective, present and future, structure and process' (1996: 15). Law (1996a) agrees, suggesting that 'career' as a socially constructed concept is concerned with the processes of continuous learning, the development of new skills, the integration of personal, family and social dimensions, an attitude of open-mindedness, and a clear but flexible sense of direction.

In terms of current practice in careers work, there is a growing recognition that our understanding of 'career' needs to be both inclusive, embracing the multiple dimensions of the lives of all individuals, and exclusive, promoting learning about the world of work, community and adult life. For Collin (1996), the power of careers education and guidance lies in the capacity to link the private world of the individual to the economic and social structure. For policy makers 'career' is 'sufficiently wedded to the work ethic to hold considerable potential for social control, and yet also sufficiently flexible to allow room for alternative sources of meaning, social and cultural differences, and self respect' (1996: 15). For Watts the 'new' concept returns career to the dictionary definition as 'the individual's lifelong progression in learning and in work' (1999: 2), thus placing learning at the centre of career development theory, and career at the heart of the wider agenda of education and lifelong learning. For practitioners, such a reconstruction of careers presents many challenges to careers education and guidance practice.

For many schools and colleges, careers education, careers information and guidance provision have historically been based upon a model of career that emphasises providing information and learning about employing organisations and career hierarchies. In such instances, the understanding of 'career' is inextricably linked to learning about jobs, and primacy is given to the act of 'choosing a career' in what is conceived of as a relatively stable labour market. The breakdown of traditional certainties about and patterns of employment questions the notion of career, and challenges careers practitioners to develop more fluid approaches, stressing the lifetime development of 'career management skills' (SCAA, 1996). Careers coordinators and curriculum managers need to find ways of addressing the notion of 'career' as a personal, subjective, socially constructed reality, an approach that necessitates greater interaction with the community, and the incorporation of individual and community aspirations and concerns into the design and delivery of careers provision.

What is careers education?

Having explored the changing concept and reality of 'career' we now need to explore how careers education and guidance are defined and delivered in the curriculum of schools and colleges in England.

Careers education in England is not a subject as defined by the National Curriculum; it is an 'aspect' of the curriculum that is usually taught in secondary schools as a subject. Careers education has no clearly defined or agreed body of knowledge and no national programme of study. Everyone has an opinion of what careers education and guidance purport to be about, and yet there is no consensus of understanding in the educational community. All schools and colleges deliver careers education and guidance, but few careers coordinators or other teachers are aware of the theoretical rationales that underpin the different aspects of their teaching programmes. All students 'do' careers education and guidance in schools and colleges, but few can clearly articulate what the programme was trying to achieve. It is often argued that all teachers teach 'careers', but in reality few teachers are conscious of this!

As with the term 'career', our understanding of the terms 'careers education' and 'careers guidance' is problematic. As Harris (1999) points out, both of these terms are contested and ambiguous, and can be understood in a number of ways according to the ideology of the particular person, school, college or other 'stakeholder' organisation concerned. This lack of a clear meaning and consensus of understanding is as true amongst school careers coordinators as it is amongst non-careers specialists. When asked to define the term 'careers education and guidance', newly appointed careers coordinators demonstrate a wide range of understanding about the term. The following word associations are frequently attributed to the term: 'making choices', 'progression for the future', 'giving information about jobs', 'next steps', 'world of work', 'opportunities', 'learning about work', 'planning', 'achieving own potential', 'individual responsibility', 'making decisions'. The multiple meanings and conflicting rationales for an aspect of the curriculum that has been in place in most schools for over a quarter of a century betray the depth of the ambiguity. Bates (1984) suggests that this ambiguity has been both a strength and a weakness for careers work in schools. Strength has been derived from the fact that careers education and guidance have been flexible enough to change, survive, adapt and prosper in a sometimes hostile political and educational climate during the past 25 years. Thus careers education and guidance have been appropriated by various political, social, economic, educational and cultural interests at different times, and utilising different rationales to further their causes. Careers practitioners and service managers have attempted to hitch the careers education and guidance wagon to many curriculum initiatives in order to ensure survival, and further the status and place of careers work and guidance services in education and the community. However, the malleability of careers education and guidance as a concept has also proved a source of weakness and vulnerability. Harris (1999) points to the sense of philosophical incoherence and lack of understanding in the educational community about careers work. In practice, this lack of coherence has resulted in feelings of frustration amongst many careers practitioners about changing government policy for careers work, and the impact on the careers curriculum and guidance practice, including amongst those employed by organisations who have benefited from the increase in status and resources for careers work in education.

Creating an environment to enable individuals to learn about themselves, and to connect their developing ideas, needs and aspirations to the adult world, is at the heart of careers education and careers guidance within education. Students who are engaged with careers education and careers guidance processes frequently cite this personal 'it's about me' focus as the key reason why careers work is so important to them. The capacity to give space, time, attention, respect and recognition to the developing ideas, concerns, needs and beliefs of young people marks careers work out as different to the traditional transmission processes operating through much of the mainstream curriculum. As Watts (1996b) suggests, careers education and guidance operate 'at the interface between the individual and society, between self and opportunity, between aspiration and realism'.

Within much curriculum policy literature, the term 'careers education and guidance' is used to denote those aspects of the curriculum that help young people to develop the skills, knowledge, understanding and attitudes required to prepare for and to progress through adult life including continuing education and employment. The aims for careers education and guidance policies and provision in schools and colleges are articulated in this discourse, usually in terms of developing students' decision making skills, opportunity awareness, transition learning and self-awareness. This so-called DOTS analysis formulated by Bill Law and Tony Watts (1977) has remained a foundation stone for careers education and guidance practice for over 20 years. Many schools have later incorporated the Schools Curriculum and Assessment Authority (SCAA) refinement of DOTS as the basis of their careers policies and provision. The SCAA document *Looking Forward: Careers Education and Guidance in the Curriculum* (1995) formulated the aims into a three-stage linear process of learning about self, opportunities and taking action. The three aims were stated as helping pupils to:

1 understand themselves and develop their capabilities
2 investigate careers and opportunities
3 implement their career plans.

More recently, the Qualifications and Curriculum Authority has further cemented these three aims by attaching the headings 'self-development', 'career exploration' and 'career management' to aims 1, 2 and 3 respectively (QCA, 1999).

For most teachers who are aware of this curriculum guidance, their understanding of the purposes of careers education and guidance correlates to their broader understanding of the purposes of education, and of teaching and learning. This understanding of careers education places it at the heart of the education process. The new National Curriculum document reinforces this message, clearly locating career learning and the preparation for work and adult life within the broader statement of aims, values and purposes of education:

[The curriculum] should give them [pupils] the opportunity to become creative, innovative, enterprising and capable of leadership to equip them for their future lives as workers and citizens . . . It should prepare pupils for the next steps in their education, training and employment and equip them to make informed choices at school and throughout their lives, enabling them to appreciate the relevance of their achievements to life and society outside school, including leisure, community engagement and employment. (DfEE/QCA, 2000b: 10)

In most schools, the provision of careers education and guidance consists of two linked components defined by the SCAA as follows:

Careers education provides a means of developing individuals' knowledge, understanding and experience of opportunities in education, training, and employment and the skills necessary to make informed decisions. Careers guidance provides a means of helping individuals to apply relevant knowledge, understanding and skills to their own particular circumstances when choices have to be made. (1995: 7)

Law (1996b) rightly suggests that the distinction drawn here between careers education and careers guidance is arbitrary and false, and has simply served as an administrative convenience to mark the professional territorial boundaries and responsibilities of education institutions and the Careers Service. By their nature, careers education and careers guidance should be integrated processes that contribute to the careers learning of students, rather than distinctive or exclusive 'parallel' processes (see Morris et al., 2000).

Thus far we have used official government policy documents to arrive at a broad definition of the curriculum aims for careers education and guidance. Below this surface level, the policy rationales and context of careers education and guidance are highly politicised and contested.

Policy agenda for careers education in schools and colleges

The discourse of careers education and careers guidance has been the subject for extensive analysis and debate within the careers and education research community (see Barnes and Andrews, 1995; Harris, 1999; Stacey and Mignot, 2000; Watts, 1996b). At the level of policy, the past 25 years have seen careers education and careers guidance appropriated by a range of governmental, business and community interests, to be used as a way of promoting myriad political, social and economic goals. At the governmental and business level, careers work has been a component in the strategy to ensure that the education, training and labour markets are efficiently geared to support the aims of economic competitiveness in a global market. Influenced by interest groups such as the Confederation for British Industry (CBI, 1989; 1993a; 1993b), the political and economic rationale for careers work in education has been located in the policy discourse of inclusion and employability, articulated in terms of individual qualifications attainment, skills development and preparedness and capability for employment. As a consequence of this interest, careers education and guidance have been a core component within a series of vocational education and training curriculum initiatives designed to address youth unemployment, skills shortages, economic competitiveness and the employability of youth. Whilst it will be argued that the economic discourse appears to have been the dominant one, it has not been homogeneous, or uncontested.

For our purposes, four interrelated policy imperatives will be identified to help in the analysis of the place and purpose of careers education and guidance in education.

Economic imperatives

As we have shown, the policy goals for careers education and guidance have historically been directed to address social, cultural and economic issues arising from changes in technology, the economy or the labour market. Much early post-war careers work focused on helping young people to develop broad vocational skills and then to find jobs that would be suitable for them in an era of near universal employment. Economic imperatives provided the main driving force for the raising of the school leaving age (ROSLA) with the introduction of work experience in 1974, the introduction of a national Careers Service from 1974, and for pre-vocational and career-related work arising from the rise in youth unemployment from the mid 1970s. 'Special measures' in education continued through the 1980s and 1990s including the TVEI programme (1983–97), Compacts (1988) and education–business 'partnerships' (1989) with the goal of bringing the outputs of the education system into closer correspondence to the needs of business (see Killeen et al., 1992). Careers education and guidance played a central role within these educational initiatives, supporting student decision making and smoothing transitions in order to address the perceived skills need of business. This policy rationale culminated in the interdepartmental *Competitiveness* White Papers (DfEE, 1995; DTI, 1994) and the OFSTED/Audit Commission *Unfinished Business* (1992) report.

The policy strategy of the 1997 New Labour government for social inclusion through economic participation maintained a significant strand of the previous administration's approach to education. From 1998 the DfEE commenced the process of 'refocusing' the Careers Service to work more with the so-called 'disaffected', and thereby to support the achievement of the national learning targets of progression into approved forms of learning and work. The policy goals of inclusion through employability (Hillage and Pollard, 1998), the rational deployment of human resources, and the efficient operation of the market mechanism form the bedrock of this Labour government's policy frame for careers work, and this continues to provide a key justification for continued funding of the Careers Service, and for school policies for inclusion and raising achievement.

Educational imperatives

The educational imperatives for careers education and guidance demonstrate a close link to the economic rationale. The focusing of schools and
colleges on targets for attainment, progress, retention and inclusion has cast
guidance and careers education processes as part of a helping mechanism
that will provide stimulus for engaging students in learning, to stay in
the mainstream education system, and to be motivated to achieve, attain
and progress into approved learning options. This philosophy imbues
early programmes to address unemployment and skills shortages such as
TVEI, CPVE and pre-vocational courses including GNVQ. More recently
Excellence in Schools (DfEE, 1997a), *Careers Education and Guidance in Schools*
(DfEE, 1997c), and the *Learning Age* (DfEE, 1999e) have all restated this
rationale and vision for careers education and guidance:

> Careers education and guidance can help all young people achieve their potential
> . . . Careers education and guidance can raise the aspirations of those with limited
> horizons. It can increase motivation and achievement of those at risk of losing
> their way. (DfEE, 1997c)

National learning targets, school/college attainment league tables, raising
achievement, school improvement and inclusion targets all highlight the
need for guidance to ensure that students engage and progress within
the system. In this context, guidance is viewed as a motivating force linked
to target setting, pupil review and achievement in key skills, and with the
wider policy goals of participation in learning and employability. Many
'disaffection' projects and targeted programmes of 'alternative curriculum'
and work-related learning in Key Stage 4 are rooted in this employability
policy goal. The strategy document *Connexions: the Best Start in Life for Every
Young Person* (DfEE, 2000a) and the new citizenship framework (DfEE/
QCA, 2000c) demonstrate this adherence to economic and social integration,
social cohesion and inclusion through citizenship and employment.

Personal development imperative

The goal of supporting the personal autonomy of the individual has
been at the heart of humanist approaches to careers work in the UK, and
remains a central tenet within the training programmes for careers advisers.
Many careers guidance practitioners and teachers strongly believe in
humanist, developmental and self-concept approaches to inform careers
education and guidance work, with the goal of empowering the individual
to make choices for themselves, as independent from their social, economic,
political or cultural context as possible. The 'developmental' approach of the
American psychologists Donald Super (1957) and Eli Ginzberg (1972) have
been extremely influential in this respect, building on the foundations for
humanistic counselling laid by Carl Rogers (1961). There continues to be
much power in these ideas, and significant good in promoting the idea of

the individual as a developing person, and as a sovereign and free agent. This approach remains vitally important within the evolving rationales for careers education and guidance work in schools and colleges

On the more negative side, the rhetoric of personal responsibility, individual empowerment and free choice were appropriated as part of the Thatcherite policy discourse of the 1980s. Individual choice provided an ideological mantra for the Conservative right, but also provided legitimation for careers education and guidance as an aspect of the curriculum that aimed at promoting skills of decision making and choice without having to attend to the social, economic or cultural contexts of individual students. Aspects of this policy theme have been appropriated by the New Labour government, persisting through the rhetoric of lifelong learning and lifelong career development. However, Ken Roberts (1977; 1981; 1994) and Bill Law (1984; 1996a) have criticised the pure humanistic approach as conceptually naïve, and affirmed the important role of community and socio-economic context in helping to shape and construct personal identity and aspirations. For Roberts, Law and others the idea of individual sovereignty and choice free of social and cultural context is problematic, and potentially open to forms of practice that problematise and disregard young people and their communities and cultures. As Edwards et al. (1998) suggests, within the rhetoric of 'lifelong learning', individual responsibility and choice are used as political mechanisms to divorce the individual's behaviour and achievements from their wider social, cultural or economic context. As a consequence, any blame for non-achievement and non-participation is deflected away from the state to the individual or their parents.

Social/cultural imperatives

The social/cultural imperative for careers education and guidance is to promote the goals of social inclusion, social justice, equal opportunities and community citizenship. In this context, careers work aims to secure community ownership and support of provision and services, and to base careers work on a value set of recognition and respect for the individual and cultural differences. The priority for careers education and guidance is to establish the structures and provision that individuals need, and that are relevant to the real lives and situations of individuals. The potential for this rationale is that it affords the opportunity to design provision that deproblematises the idea of youth, that sees young people, their lives, backgrounds and cultures as positive resources, and which works to engage individuals in their own solutions and future development.

The priorities for careers education and guidance provision are to be relevant to young people and their communities, to establish strategies that challenge the status quo in the distribution of opportunities in education and the labour market, and to help young people to optimise their life chances and choices, and to achieve their own potential in realistic but equitable ways. Provision needs to help individuals develop the skills and knowledge to access and make best use of the opportunities open to them, according to their own needs and desires, but within a positive context of recognition and regard for the aspirations and concerns of the students' family, culture and community.

Careers practice should contribute to a redistributivist approach to social justice, attempting to target additional and community resources on disadvantaged individuals and groups to help address inequalities of background gender, race and disability. Whilst it has been argued that the government's social inclusion strategy is primarily concerned with social and economic integration, there is potential for the development of a proactive community and needs-based service through Connexions. The approach for an integrated guidance service outlined in *Bridging the Gap* (SEU, 1999) and the Connexions strategy document *Connexions: the Best Start in Life for Every Young Person* (DfEE, 2000a), and supported by the implementation of the new foundation subject of citizenship to be taught in schools from 2002 (see *Citizenship in Key Stages 3 and 4*, DfEE/QCA, 2000c) could provide a framework for a community-based service. The need for Connexions service policy, design and governance to secure the active involvement of a partnership of young people, the community, and the schools and colleges is paramount. To quote recent guidance produced by the National Youth Agency on behalf of the DfEE:

> Young people will soon become disillusioned with limited and/or ineffectual approaches to involving them with the Connexions Service. A thorough approach to engaging young people is required which pays attention to management and delivery issues including strategy, values, culture, structures, processes, systems and the skills and attitudes of staff. Young people need to be involved at all levels of the Service, from national down to the very local. They need to be able to contribute effectively to the many different aspects of the work and their representation needs to reflect the diversity of communities – in terms of place, culture, values, interests, ability, gender, class, race – to which young people belong. (NYA/DfEE, 2000)

There is an agenda here for careers education and guidance in supporting social and cultural justice, participation and development, as well as developing provision that supports individual growth and development. The underpinning rationale for careers education and guidance in education needs to be rearticulated to better balance the needs of individuals and communities with those of the funding agencies, governments and businesses. A rationale that respects and celebrates difference and community is needed. We will return to these issues in the final section of this chapter.

What is the place of careers education in the curriculum?

Thus far our discussion has focused on how 'career' is being reconceptualised to emphasise the individual and the personal, rather than objective organisational and labour market realities. Our discussion has also attended to the range of underpinning rationales for careers education and guidance provision in schools and colleges in England. The extent to which current provision of careers education and guidance is developing to respond to the reconceptualisation of 'career' at the level of practice is questionable. As Harris (1999) has shown, it is also questionable whether most schools and college careers programmes are consciously founded on coherent theoretical rationales. We will return to these themes later to explore some of the options for change in careers education and guidance in the twenty-first century.

Research has shown that the experience of career learning and development for many students is of relatively traditional and mechanistic approaches, with programmes aimed at providing opportunity information and forcing students through a process of decision making about their next steps at 16 or 18, rather than a broader approach to the development of critical research faculties, key skills and career management skills (Morris et al., 2000; NACGT, 1999; OFSTED, 1998a; 1998b). Careers education and guidance for many students are still front-loaded in their final years of compulsory schooling, rather than a service to support career development throughout life. Many schools and colleges have constructed careers programmes from a range of activities and materials, and assumptions about 'what works'. As Harris (1999) shows, programmes tend to be constructed more on the basis of pragmatism than on theory, and as a result may use teaching and learning methods or activities that are predicated upon different and sometimes contradictory theoretical rationales.

Since 1945, careers education has occupied a peripheral and contested place in the curriculum of schools and colleges in the UK. Careers education and guidance have existed as an aspect of the students' curriculum in most secondary schools for over 25 years, as a subject taught by careers coordinators and other careers 'specialists' within the personal and social education (PSE) programme, or as a separately timetabled subject. The teaching of careers education has conformed to the traditional 'front-loading' model for education which deems that students need to have made a well-informed and final decision about their future, and to have implemented their plans by the time they are 16 years of age. As a consequence, most formally taught careers education and careers guidance takes place with school students in the statutory phase of Years 9 to 11. Careers education rarely has the same status as academic subjects within schools. In nearly three-quarters of secondary schools careers education makes up a series of distinct modules within the PSE programme (NACGT, 1999; OFSTED, 1998a). During the past 25 years careers education and guidance practitioners and theorists have failed to attract sufficient support to establish careers education as a subject worthy of inclusion in the core or foundation National Curriculum, and thereby establish a strong subject-based profession for careers teachers. As a consequence, in many schools and colleges, lip service has been paid to the real needs of students regarding careers education and guidance, with careers education being 'lumped' with a rag-bag of other low-status and non-assessed aspects of the curriculum to form part of personal and social education, 'life skills' or college 'tutorial enrichment' programmes.

Most primary schools do not formally recognise that careers education and guidance form part of their school curriculum, although as Law and McGowan (1999) suggest, much career-related learning takes place in primary phase education as a natural part of teaching and learning about self, community and the world of work, recognised or not. More recently, the important place and role of career-related learning in primary schools as an essential element of personal, social and health education (PSHE) have been recognised in the non-statutory guidelines for PSHE (DfEE/QCA, 2000b) and in the supporting guidance to schools (DfEE, 2000f). In colleges of further education the position is also variable, with careers usually being taught as a part of mainstream vocational courses, or through the tutorial or enrichment curriculum, or through optional workshop and seminar programmes complemented by the provision of individual guidance coordinated through tutors or central student services departments.

Goodson (1988) argues that the marginalisation of aspects of the curriculum such as careers education has been derived from its non-inclusion in the 'liberal' subject patterns inherited from the universities and public and grammar schools of the nineteenth century. He argues that the high-status subjects of the current National Curriculum are essentially the same as those included in the list of 'acceptable' subjects formally embodied in the regulations of 1904 and the 1917 School Certificate. These subjects have been retained, reproduced and defended by the vested career interests of the teacher subject associations, the universities and the educational establishment. Through such processes, vocational, careers and work-related learning have been effectively excluded from the mainstream curriculum, with a consequent low status ascribed by the system to careers teachers and teachers of 'vocational' aspects of the curriculum. In most schools, it has only been relatively recently that careers education programmes have been subject to the same rigours of planning, review, assessment, evaluation and reporting as mainstream curriculum subjects. Their very informality further mitigated against the recognition by teachers and students of careers education as a serious endeavour.

In spite of this, the place of careers education and guidance has evolved, and the status and profile have improved significantly over time. Law (1996b) argues that the evolution of careers education and guidance provision in schools can be seen as a response to changing economic, technological and labour market circumstances. He identifies three historical periods for careers education and guidance: first, an optional and *ad hoc* information and job placing service for early leavers, provided by schools and the Youth Employment Service (1910–70); second, careers as an optional part of the curriculum with careers guidance provided by the new Careers Service (1970–82); and third, careers education and guidance as compulsory, backed up by a professional information and placing service for all young people (1983–present). Harris (1999) categorises this process of evolution in terms of four careers education 'paradigms': until the 1950s careers guidance services aimed at 'matching talents' and 'finding jobs', and from the 1960s careers education and guidance aimed to 'produce workers' and then to 'develop citizens'. Harris argues that these changing paradigms for careers education can be viewed as a response to the economic, technological, political and labour market changes described in Chapter 1.

Curriculum guidance

The welter of policy guidance (NACGT, 2000) to schools and colleges on how they can promote and develop careers education and guidance within, around and sometimes in spite of the National Curriculum has continued unabated since *Working Together for a Better Future* (DES/DE, 1987). At no time, however, has careers education been viewed as a significant aspect of the mainstream curriculum in many schools. The curriculum location of careers education has varied over time, between schools, and between different parts of the country. In many schools and colleges it continues to be a contested part of the curriculum. Structurally, careers education and guidance have moved from being a stand-alone subject or part of PSE (1980s), to a National Curriculum cross-curricular theme (early 1990s), to a non-statutory curriculum 'entitlement' (DTI, 1994; SCAA, 1995), to a statutory aspect of the curriculum with links to PSHE and citizenship (DfEE, 1997b; DfEE/QCA, 2000b).

The response from many schools and colleges has been pragmatic. Evidence has shown that the place of careers education usually varies according to the prevailing priorities of the senior managers and governors, the resources and time available, and the understanding and 'ethos' of the school regarding careers and personal development (Morris et al., 2000). In some schools careers education is clearly located within the context of personal and social development and pastoral care. In others it is a function of work-related or vocational education curriculum. In others still, it remains a discrete part of the curriculum with its own departmental values and teaching delivery framework, and may also incorporate other aspects of the PSE and work-related curriculum. The interrelationships and overlaps between careers education provision and that of work experience and work-related education, personal and social education (PSE), guidance, recording achievement, and the various vocational education initiatives often betray a deep sense of confusion amongst policy makers, teachers, parents/carers and students (this sense of confusion experienced by students can be identified in the views of students: see DfEE, 1998a; Morris et al., 2000). This sense of confusion exacerbates the low regard for careers work held by many students and teachers.

Until 1997, careers education and guidance largely existed as a voluntary aspect of the curriculum in schools, or was included in response to the financial or contractual inducements of educational initiatives and programmes such as TVEI (1983–97), the Year 9/10 Careers Initiative (1994–7) and the Work Experience Initiative (1994 onwards). From 1997, the requirement for schools to deliver careers education and guidance became a statutory obligation through the Education Act (DfEE, 1997b). The three clauses contained within the Act require schools to provide careers education, careers information and access to the Careers Service for students in Years 9–11, and this Act secured the place of careers education, information and guidance in the curriculum. However, the legislation has not required schools to do very much. There is no requirement in terms of minimum curriculum time, programme aims and objectives, content, resourcing or staffing allocation. The lack of 'teeth' within the legislation has been exacerbated by the cursory handling of careers education and guidance within the revised OFSTED framework for the inspection of schools (OFSTED, 1999). In the revised framework, inspectors are merely required to 'evaluate and report on the quality and range (and effectiveness) of opportunities for learning provided by the school for all pupils, highlighting features which are particular strengths and weaknesses . . . including specific comment on . . . Work-related education, including careers education and guidance for all secondary age pupils' (in line with OFSTED guidance: OFSTED, 1998c). Recent research in this area (Harris, 1999; Morris et al., 2000; NACGT, 1999) clearly demonstrates that whilst there have been significant improvements, there remains wide variation in the status, content, organisation and curriculum time allocated to careers work between schools, and in different parts of the country.

The revised National Curriculum (DfEE/QCA, 2000b) re-emphasises the statutory obligations for schools, although it structurally reinforces the marginal place of careers education and guidance within curriculum arrangements. The revision of the non-statutory framework for personal, social and health education (PSHE) (DfEE/QCA, 2000a) together with the increased flexibilities for disapplication in Key Stage 4, and the requirements for schools to introduce the new foundation subject of citizenship from 2002, pose additional challenges to the future role and coherence of careers education as a viable aspect in a crowded curriculum. Without a coherent programme of study within the National Curriculum, or clear requirements for inspection and quality assurance, for many schools and colleges careers education remains at the periphery of the 'serious' curriculum.

A further area of concern in terms of both policy and practice is the lack of agreement about the content of a careers education programme, with no national programme of study for schools and colleges setting out a coherent body of knowledge or agreed sets of skills to be developed. The lack of a programme of study remains a serious weakness for those practitioners wishing to promote the cause of careers education, careers guidance and work-related learning in schools and colleges. At present there are several sources of non-statutory guidance from the DfEE and QCA that provide clues about the content and methodology for the design and teaching delivery of careers education and guidance (NACGT, 2000).

Following conventional practice taking place in most schools in the mid 1990s, the components of a 'good' careers education programme were initially identified by the National Curriculum Council (NCC, 1991) and later by the Schools Curriculum Assessment Authority in the paper *Looking Forward: Careers Education and Guidance in the Curriculum* (SCAA, 1995). The five curriculum 'components' of a 'good' careers education and guidance programme in schools were identified thus:

1 a taught programme of careers-related courses and activities
2 continuing guidance including careers guidance
3 accurate information including careers information
4 experience of work including work experience
5 action planning and recording achievement.

Three of the five components outlined were legislated as entitlements for students in Years 9–11 in the three clauses of the 1997 Education Act that apply to careers education and guidance, although suggested learning aims and objectives for these programmes were not specified. Work experience and recording achievement have no legislative requirement, although in most schools forms of provision will be made in these areas.

In 1999, the QCA published suggested *Learning Outcomes from Careers Education and Guidance*. The document was intended to provide greater clarity for the aims and objectives of careers education in Key Stages 3 and 4 and post-16, and to promote the notion that school and college careers education and guidance programmes should be written in a prescriptive learning outcomes format.

Careers education remains part of the 'Cinderella' curriculum in many schools and colleges, and although careers education has increased in profile, it has not uniformly done so. By turn its place in the curriculum has been secured by the perception of school and college senior managers and careers coordinators that students need support with career learning, and by its current popularity as an aspect of government public policy which ensures that schools and colleges are pressured to respond to a mixture of legislative requirements, curriculum guidance, the demands of funding bodies and OFSTED inspection requirements. As Morris et al. (2000) suggest, the status and profile of careers education in schools are invariably a function of the emphasis given to it by senior managers, and the status of the careers coordinators working in the schools. Many school careers coordinators design and deliver career work pragmatically according to a number of factors: the time and resources available to them, the require-ments on them laid down by their senior managers, the interest and enthusiasm for the subject of the careers coordinator, and the level of project support and funding available from external organisations such as the LEA or the Careers Service. As a result, progress in schools is slow and success has been patchy. Repeated surveys have shown (NACGT; 1989; 1999; NACGT/ICG, 1993; 1996; OFSTED 1995; 1998a; 1999) that there have been specific improvements in careers work in secondary schools, but that wide variations persist between schools and colleges in the quality of provision, with careers work still operating as a 'bolt-on' to the rest of the curriculum.

Higher education

Higher education has undergone radical change in the last two decades. Full-time graduate enrolments doubled between 1979–93, while part time numbers increased by 160 per cent in the same period (Purcell and Pitcher, 1996). More women, mature students and students from ethnic minorities are now in higher education; at the same time, the nature of the graduate job has altered (Purcell et al., 1999). Higher Education Careers Service has had to adapt to these changing circumstances, largely without the benefit of extra staff. This adaptation has also been shaped by government policy, first from 1987, when the Enterprise in Higher Education (EHE) initiative began and ten years later, when the Dearing Report was published (National Commission of Enquiry into Higher Education, 1997).

The EHE initiative provided additional funding for innovations in teaching and learning, with a focus on the improvement of specific capabilities in students. Over a period of five years (1987–1992), over 60 H.E. institutions received about one million pounds each, with twenty thousand employers and one million students involved in projects. The purpose of the Initiative was to foster change in H.E. and this was manifested in various ways such as career and skill based workshops, mentored work experience, learning contracts, and self, peer and team assessment. However, as Hawkins and Winter (1997) observe change needed to be more than superficial to make a real difference to careers education in H.E.

Evaluation of the programmes (Hustler et al., 1998; Watts and Hawthorn, 1992) indicate substantial changes in the way careers education has been developed in H.E. The notion of career management skills has become widely accepted as a focus for such programmes; career management means a number of things such as taking control of one's personal development, as well as making career choices, and it overlaps with personal transferable skills. Hustler et al. (1998) found a wide range of delivery practices being offered, from modules integrated into a degree, to one off 'special' events. They distinguished between the module approach, which could be generic or customised, the integrated approach and the extra curricular approach. With the module approach, the careers service has a key role in delivery but there can be a danger of this approach being marginalised and skill development not applying to the rest of the curriculum. In the case of the integrated approach, career management skills should be more central to the whole curriculum requiring a close partnership between career and academic staff, as well as employers and students making new and heavy demands on careers services. The extra curricular approach involves special events such as careers fairs but these run the risk of 'tokenism'.

Evidence from Watts and Hawthorn (1992) and Hustler et al. (1998) suggest that career management skills programmes stemming from the EHE initiative have been successful for a number of reasons. These include positive student feedback, employer links, more graduates in work, the growing emphasis on a broader skills and learning development agenda and external imperatives such as Teaching Quality Assessment. Factors that have inhibited the success of such programmes are: pressure on academics in other directions such as research, the inflexibility of some modular systems, limited employer contact, a squeeze on funding and lukewarm support from senior managers. What clearly emerges is the need to reposition the role of the Careers Service in the light of its new role, and there are several alternatives which include the service acting more as consultants or where careers staff provide teaching to departments at a cost. Hustler et al. (1998) identity a major staff development issue facing universities, resulting from the need to deliver effective career management skills modules.

Hawkins and Winter (1997) and Watts and Hawthorn (1992) agree that the EHE initiative has challenged the traditional model of Higher Education. It has offered a radical alternative, putting student services at the centre of teaching and learning. This has been reinforced by the Dearing Report (1997), which produced a number of far reaching recommendations with regard to the provision of careers education, work experience, employer contact and student profiling. At the same time, Watts (1997) suggested a number of possible models for the development of careers work in H.E. The curriculum model defined careers services as becoming part of a delivery vehicle designed to support academic departments in incorporating employability skills and career management skills into course provision. This is the model most H.E. careers services are adopting, whether or not they were a part of the EHE initiative. McChesney (1995) explored the development and evaluation of careers education programmes in H.E. She found that students value them as part of their course, although, for some, they were seen as marginal. In considering careers staff, McChesney observed that new skills in teaching and an understanding of developmental theory were necessary.

The changes set in motion over a decade ago are now established throughout H.E. The need for a comprehensive careers education programme is accepted as an integral part of a student's experience. Linking career to personal and academic development is also perceived as essential by a growing number of universities, as evidenced by the Personal and Academic development of students in Higher Education programme (PADSHE). This project began in 1996 and was funded by the Higher

Education Funding Council. It provides tutors and students with a developmental framework for focusing on the various needs of students, and should enable a holistic approach. Both this initiative and career management skills modules are becoming available electronically.

Where next for careers education and guidance?

The previous sections have demonstrated that the status and place of careers education and guidance in the curriculum have historically been insecure and contested. Careers education is critically vulnerable to changes of policy at the government level or school level, and suffers from lack of clarity in terms of conceptual coherence, and in terms of any agreement over what careers curriculum provision would be adequate to meet the needs of young people. The driving force for careers education and guidance policy has been for too long articulated within the discourse of economic competitiveness, relegating careers education and guidance practice to act as a political lubricant for national social and economic policy (Watts, 1996b). In practice, careers education and guidance have relied on the largely unrecognised commitment and enthusiasm of school careers coordinators operating at the margins of the curriculum, supported by external careers advisers from the Careers Service. The net result has been a pragmatic processing model of careers work designed to provide the bare essentials of information and guidance needed for young people to address decision points, and to force students through a system of officially approved 'learning' gateways and transition points. The minimalism of this approach has paid too little attention to the personal, social and cultural growth and development of individuals and has failed to make a significant contribution to help redress the myriad social, economic and cultural inequalities. This has been the tragedy for an aspect of the curriculum that by its nature should aim to engage with young people on their terms, about their real life concerns, and in their real communities. However, the current political and educational environment presents a number of opportunities that could help to address some of these historic problems and issues, and take forward careers education and guidance as an integrated service at the heart of the curriculum.

Curriculum change

Changes taking place in the 14–19 curriculum in schools and colleges present a number of opportunities to develop a framework for a coherent, progressive and 'personal' careers and guidance provision. The requirements of the new National Curriculum necessitate the review of arrangements in primary and secondary schools for personal, social and health education, the introduction of the new foundation subject of citizenship in secondary schools from September 2002, and school strategies for inclusion (DfEE/

QCA, 2000c). Careers education 'is concerned specifically with helping pupils to prepare for their roles as learners and workers. Decisions about learning and work, however, have implications for other life roles, particularly as family members and as consumers. Careers education, PSHE and citizenship, therefore are closely related' (DfEE/QCA, 2000b). The future arrangements for careers education and work-related learning need to be considered in relation to PSHE and citizenship in order to develop a philosophically consistent 'Life-relevant curriculum' (Law, 2000). The opportunity now exists to design a curriculum that links personal, social, health, career, family and community learning and development together. The new PSHE and citizenship reviews also present opportunities to develop a careers curriculum that recognises and draws upon students' career learning achievements gained during the primary phase of education, and thereby to ensure greater continuity and progression throughout schooling. The potential of this linkage between careers, PSHE and citizenship teaching and learning is immense. An integrated approach could provide for a more holistic, person-centred and community-centred curriculum in schools. This could form a curriculum basis for both practical and radical action at local level to address issues of social justice/injustice within communities and local education and labour markets, and at the same time to address contemporary political and economic concerns about social inclusion and raising achievement.

The extension of 'disapplication' for the purposes of work-related learning and other forms of experimental 'alternative curriculum' in Key Stage 4 (QCA, 2000) provide the basis for a future breakpoint in the National Curriculum at 14, with a broader, more flexible Key Stage 4 based around a mixture of academic, pre-vocational and occupational learning. The post-16 qualifications framework introduced from September 2000 offers further pointers towards the possibilities of a broader, unitised and needs-based curriculum, with greater recognition for vocational programmes, and closer correspondence of the academic and the vocational in terms of esteem and exchange value. The scenario of a 14–19 unitised curriculum, mixing the traditional 'academic' disciplines with vocational, community and work-related subjects, designed in a unitised framework, and negotiated as individualised learning packages with students from age 14, could provide a model for future curriculum development, and one that is currently under consideration. Such a curriculum would have huge implications for the 'flexibility' of teaching and learning, and also need to have guidance and career development at its heart, enabling students to develop career management skills and negotiate their progression. Student guidance, mentoring and support in order to negotiate learning goals and processes, to recognise achievements, to ensure the integration of learning in and out of school, and to explore the implications for personal and career learning and development would all be paramount.

Teaching and learning

Future careers education and guidance needs to be designed in order to meet the identified needs of students. This would require a flexible and differentiated provision that allows students to do different things, in different ways, and leading to different outcomes according to their individual needs. Whilst the quality standards movement has been important in stressing that careers work needs to be outcomes based, of rigorous design, and subject to the processes of monitoring, assessment, review and evaluation, it is also important for careers education to be needs based, flexible and creative. The greater individualisation and customisation of careers education and guidance and work-related learning programmes, the use of IT and 'flexible' teaching and learning methods geared towards individuals and small groups, and tutorial-based recognition and recording of achievement processes provide an agenda for development in both schools and colleges. The use of the progress files 'portfolio approach' to life development planning could provide a practical basis for integrating the processes of career planning, academic target setting and review, and personal development planning, and could underpin the development of a differentiated careers education and guidance provision at the level of the student.

The teaching of careers work also needs to be more radical, risk-taking and creative in approaches to teaching and learning, and to be about helping students to think new things and gain exciting new experiences. Some of the creative approaches currently being taken by schools, colleges, youth services and careers services in schools and colleges and as part of the Learning Gateway to work with the so-called 'at-risk' or 'disaffected' provide examples of approaches that can be used in order to engage students in career-related learning (see Hughes, 2000). Many of these approaches are concerned with personal, social or career-related learning made relevant through a culture of individual and community recognition, utilising the medium of group, community or work-related settings for learning and supported by opportunities for individual mentoring. Inter-agency working and the use of individual careers guidance methods as an integral part of the careers teaching and learning process appear to be central to these new project-based approaches. This integrative model for guidance as a part of teaching and learning should signal a way forward for careers work in schools and colleges through the emerging Connexions service.

Connexions: towards an integrated guidance provision?

Future careers education and guidance need to be more firmly rooted in both humanist and social constructionist theory, which support the principles of respect and regard for individual students but also ensure that provision is based on a recognition of the differential backgrounds, culture and values of individual students and their communities. The emergence of all-age guidance and community guidance as significant issues for lifelong learning development supported through the information, advice and guidance (IAG) networks, combined with the nascent developments regarding the Connexions service, should provide opportunities to design provision that supports the personal, social and careers growth and development of the individual, but within the context of a strategy that advocates and supports social, economic and cultural justice at the level of individual and community. In this context, schools, colleges, careers services, community organisations and Connexions development workers need to find ways of actively involving young people (see NYA/DfEE, 2000) and the communities to design careers education and guidance service and provision in education and the community that genuinely meet their needs, and that is an servant to and advocate for the interests of communities rather than the economy or the state. Connexions provides an opportunity for schools and colleges working with careers services, youth services and other organisations to take a more strategic approach towards the place and provision of guidance within education institutions, and to link this with the development of an all-age provision within communities. Through such a process, careers education and guidance provision can be designed to meet the differing needs of individuals, communities and funding organisations. The school and college curriculum context for this task will vary significantly between institutions, although as has been outlined above, there are many features of the current curriculum agenda that are supportive of such an approach.

Conclusion

In this chapter we have focused on the changing context for careers education and guidance as an aspect of the curriculum in schools and colleges. We have explored from a historical perspective both the strengths and weaknesses in the current place of careers education and guidance in the curriculum, and have considered some of the policy rationales used to underpin the purpose of careers work in education. The final section moved on to outline some of the opportunities for careers education and guidance to be revitalised as part of a broader guidance curriculum entitlement for all students. Much of this chapter has been critical of current practice. This critique is based on a passionate and personal belief that things could be so much better for young people in our schools and colleges, and that careers education and guidance could have a critical role to play in developing and supporting a needs-based, inclusive and progressive curriculum that recognises and values the achievements of all students. This task will need to involve young people, their families and communities to a much greater extent in processes of decision making about curriculum and service design. Connexions and the new qualifications framework may provide opportunities for practitioners to push forward this work, and to find ways of engaging students in their own futures and that of their communities. To paraphrase Tim Edwards (1997), if we expect young people to act like adults, to be engaged in educational processes, and to have a stake-holding in their own futures and in civil society, then we need to provide the conditions for them to participate. This will need to involve giving them the same rights, responsibilities and respect that we expect ourselves. Careers education and guidance can and should have a role to play in this important task.

7

ANTI-OPPRESSIVE PRACTICE

> There is no middle ground; intervention either adds to oppression (or at least condones it) or goes some small way towards easing or breaking such oppression. In this respect, the political slogan, 'If you're not part of the solution, you must be part of the problem', is particularly accurate. An awareness of the sociopolitical context is necessary in order to prevent becoming (or remaining) part of the problem.
>
> (Thompson, 1992: 169–0)

The nature of anti-oppressive practice

The first question that this chapter must address is: 'What is anti-oppressive practice?' Following Thompson (1997) the author provides the following definition:

> Anti-oppressive practice is based on a conscious awareness of the various forms of oppression and discrimination present within society. It involves practitioners in actively seeking opportunities to challenge and undermine sexism, racism, ageism, disabilism and other forms of oppression and discrimination that may be encountered in their day-to-day practice. This also requires the practitioner to adopt a critical view of their own and others' practice, and of the institutions within which they work.

In addressing the question of anti-oppressive practice this chapter will not examine in any detail terms such as 'race', gender, age, disability etc. This in part recognises that in adopting such an approach there is always a danger of presenting a hierarchy of oppressions. Rather, this chapter will focus on the themes common to all forms of oppression: this is consistent with the view that effective anti-oppressive requires an *integrated* approach (Thompson, 1997).

As the quote at the start of this chapter clearly indicates, effective anti-oppressive practice is founded upon the practitioner's awareness of the socio-political context of their work. The socio-economic and political nature of career helping has been a recurrent theme of the previous chapters. As we have seen, the positioning of 'career' at the interface between the citizen and the state, and between the individual and society, means that career helping is not only a personal but a profoundly *political* activity (Watts, 1996b). This means that career helpers are presented with the recurrent dilemma of reconciling client-centred values with socio-economic interests. This chapter will argue that, whilst there is no ultimate resolution to this dilemma, it needs to be engaged with through ever evolving forms of anti-oppressive practice. In what follows, the political dimension of career helping will be explored in further detail. This will be followed by a critique of the various definitions of 'equal opportunities' that have underpinned career helping over the past three decades. The chapter moves on to consider some of the contemporary theoretical and practical developments that have taken place under the rubric of *social justice*. A conceptual framework for anti-oppressive practice in the context of career helping is then presented and discussed. The chapter concludes by considering ways in which anti-oppressive practice might be developed and implemented by both practitioners and institutions.

The politics of career helping revisited

The political dimension of career helping is highly complex. As Harris (1999) has suggested, not only is career helping the site of contestation amongst a myriad of 'stakeholders', but also the very nature of career helping is fundamentally ambiguous. As we have seen in previous chapters, this ambiguity relates to the uncertainty about what constitutes 'career' *and* the expectations that practitioners and clients hold as they engage in career helping activities.

R. Edwards (1997) has identified three models of public service provision which can be used to delineate the political roles that a career helper might undertake. These are: the 'social welfare' model; the 'market' model; and the 'social redistribution' model. First, the 'social welfare' model defines the career helper as a 'professional' by virtue of having a technical expertise. This relates historically to the notion that career helping is a welfare right, delivered by personnel with a strong professional identity – professional autonomy being an important cultural value here (Watts, 1996b). In contrast the 'market' model requires the career helper to act as an 'entrepreneur'. This model relates particularly to the quasi-privatisation of the UK careers service in the mid 1990s which, in turn, has been seen as part of the wider policy agenda for deprofessionalising the public services (Pfeffer and Coote, 1991; Watts, 1996b). The market model is also designed to deconstruct still further the foundations of the social welfare model of career helping by embracing and legitimising a *profit-making ethos*. Finally, the 'social redistribution' model acknowledges the 'activist' role of the career helper. Although this model is less well defined in terms of career helping provision, it does relate to the radical ideology for career helping identified by Watts (1996b). The redistributionist model also resonates strongly with the contemporary discourse of social inclusion and the Connexions strategy. As such, the politics of redistribution will be revisited later in this chapter.

As the foregoing has indicated, Watts (1996b) has identified various ideological positions that have informed public policy in relation to career helping. According to Watts these ideologies, which mirror those to be found in the wider context of education (Sadovnik et al., 1994), are as follows:

- *Conservative* Here career helping is concerned with adapting and socialising individuals into employment roles and opportunities that are 'realistically' available to them. This is to ensure social cohesion and economic prosperity. Some emphasis is placed on the dignity of all work. The conservative ideological position on career helping emphasises *social control.*
- *Liberal* Here career helping is concerned with raising the aspirations of individuals from deprived and disadvantaged groups, thus improving the life chances of the individual. The liberal position requires the individual to adopt the dominant value system of society as opposed to their own 'subculture'. The liberal ideological position emphasises *individual change.*
- *Humanistic* Here career helping aims to make individuals aware of the full range of opportunities available, helping them to choose occupations suited to their needs and preferences. The humanist position recognises that all individuals have different values together with the validity of these differences. However, the emphasis is on raising awareness; the issue of the potential lack of opportunities is not explicitly addressed. The humanist ideological position emphasises *impartiality and choice.*
- *Radical* Here career helping is based on the recognition that inequality is perpetuated by the existing economic structure and its power relations. The radical position holds that solutions must address this structure rather than the notion of deficits in individuals or groups. The radical ideological postion emphasises *social change.*

The models of delivery identified by R. Edwards (1997) and the ideologies outlined by Watts (1996b) suggest that career helping, as with other public services, not only functions as a means of promoting social control, but also has potential to achieve structural change.

It is clear that these are not circumstances peculiar to career helping. For example, the 'market' model has been tested and promoted by successive governments across the public services – the marketisation of schooling being a particular example (Griffiths, 1998). However, the author suggests that such common circumstances amongst the public services are a potential source of strength for helpers and helping organisations of all persuasions. Indeed, the acknowledgement of a shared sense of ideological confusion and a common experience of competing policy initiatives has the potential to bring career helpers, teachers, youth and community workers, and social workers closer together – to work collaboratively on the basis of a collective interest in social justice. In this sense the Connexions strategy, rather than being a threat to 'professional' identity, provides an opportunity for helpers to radicalise their practice. This potential common bond can be found in the following position on social work practice taken by Thompson:

> Social workers can be seen as the mediators between clients and the wider state apparatus. This position of 'mediator' is a crucial one as it means that social workers are in a pivotal position in terms of the relationship between the state and its citizens. The relationship is a double-edged one consisting of elements of care and control – both potential empowerment and potential oppression. Which aspect is to the fore, which element or tendency is reinforced depends largely on the actions of the social workers concerned. (1997: 10–11)

Thus, given that career helpers mediate between citizen and state, and between individuals and the labour market, they not only have the potential to challenge oppression, but also potentially contribute to and reinforce oppression. As Thompson (1997) acknowledges, this latter tendency can be achieved in two ways: by *commission*, which entails an overt act of discrimination by the 'helper'; and *omission*, whereby oppression is unwittingly perpetuated by the helper's lack of awareness and/or action.

In the context of career helping, Wrench (1992) has identified two particular examples of the act of omission in relation to racial oppression. The first example given by Wrench is the practice of 'protective channelling', whereby young black men were 'protected' from the discriminatory practices of certain local employers by their career helpers. This entailed submitting the young men to 'sympathetic' employers, thus ensuring acceptance rather than rejection. Although Wrench acknowledged the good intentions of the career helpers concerned, nonetheless he cited this as a clear example of how racist practices within the labour market can be perpetuated. The same study found evidence of white career helpers practising on the basis of 'colour-blindness' when working with black young people. This relates to the humanist ideological position identified previously (Watts, 1996b), whereby the helper works on the basis of 'treating everyone as individuals'. As others have suggested (Bimrose, 1993; Payne and Edwards, 1996), there are particular problems associated with this humanist position, which in turn is related to professional values such as 'client-centredness' and 'impartiality'. The central problem can be expressed in the following counter-intuitive statement: 'By treating everyone as an individual I treat everyone as an equal.' This is problematic because it serves to deny the possibility that 'career' aspirations are socially constructed – that individual experience is grounded in a social system that is profoundly gendered, classed and racialised. In other words, as individuals we engage with career help from different starting points and with different levels of personal, economic and cultural resources.

A further example of the politicised, mediating role of the career helper is provided by Basit (1996). In her study of the career aspirations of British Muslim girls, Basit comments on the career helping interactions that she observed in the field:

> It was manifest in all such interviews that [the career helper's] primary role was to depress the aspirations of the adolescent Muslim girls they interviewed by channelling them towards more realistic careers. They appeared to do so without giving any concrete advice as to how these girls could realise their existent aspirations and without explaining to them why they could not do so. Careers guidance was thus apparently operating as an agency of *social control* (Watts and Herr, 1976), adapting individuals to the manpower [*sic*] requirements of the economy. (1996: 237, emphasis added)

The examples given thus far have focused on career helping at the level of the practitioner. It is important also to consider the institutional dimension of career helping in relation to anti-oppressive practice. Both, as has been suggested already, are inevitably located and influenced by the wider socio-economic and political context. Two recent studies have focused on the Careers Service in relation to its work on issues of 'race' and gender. In 1999 the Equal Opportunities Commission (EOC, 1999) commissioned research into the performance of the Careers Service in promoting gender equality. In the same year the DfEE (1999c) commissioned research into the Careers Service's work with young Muslim women. A key finding arising from the EOC-commissioned research was as follows:

> The energy with which Services pursue work on gender equality is dependent on the perceived importance of equal opportunities issues by senior staff in Careers Service companies, relative to other issues of policy and practice. In recent years, Careers Services have been encouraged to focus their help on those with disadvantage, including young people with low aspirations or at risk of dropping out. This policy has directed Careers Services' energies away from other concerns, including the relative disadvantage experienced by women in the labour market. The research findings suggest that the continuing emphasis on disaffection and underachievement threatens to impede progress which might be made in pursuing gender equality at this time. (1999: vi)

In similar vein, the DfEE-commissioned research found that:

> When examining the relationship between equal opportunity policy and the implementation and outcomes of specific practices, the current priorities of the careers services in this study are set on youth disaffection and not necessarily on promoting equal opportunities. (1999c: 6)

It is the author's view that two key issues are reflected in these findings. The first issue relates to the critical importance of having an *integrated* approach to anti-oppressive practice. As Thompson (1997) suggests, given that there are multiple oppressions, effective anti-oppressive practice has to be sensitive to the ways in which gender, 'race', class etc. interrelate. In this sense, institutions without an integrated approach to anti-oppressive practice are particularly vunerable to the vagaries of public policy development and change. It should be noted at this point that the Careers Service has been viewed as the *lubricant* of socio-economic policy (Watts, 1996a). Given that there is considerable evidence to suggest that the entire Connexions strategy (DfEE, 2000a; 2000c; 2000d) is axiomatic with this view of the function of public institutions, then there would seem to be an urgent need for those involved in the new service to be clear about their position on anti-oppressive practice. This in turn relates to the second issue that, in the author's view, is reflected in the research findings given above. It is the issue of how institutions define *equal opportunities* and how these definitions underpin policy and practice.

As Thompson (1997) has suggested, anti-oppressive practice subsumes the notions of both 'equal opportunities' and 'equality'. However, as the emphasis of both the EOC (1999) and DfEE (1999c) research indicates, Careers Service and career helping practice is premised on a set of assumptions around what constitutes 'equal opportunities', i.e. the term 'anti-oppressive practice' rarely features in the discourse of mainstream career helping provision. It is therefore necessary at this point to give consideration to the various definitions of 'equal opportunities' that have been utilised in relation to career helping over the past two decades.

Equal opportunities: policy and practice

There follows a fourfold typology of equal opportunities policy and practice within schools and colleges. The typology, which was developed by an interdisciplinary group of practitioners working within the Technical and Vocational Education Initiative (TVEI), has also been applied within career helping contexts (Employment Department, 1987). There is considerable evidence to suggest that equal opportunities policy and practice within the Careers Service is founded upon types 2 and 3, i.e. the 'open door' and 'special escalator' approaches (DfEE, 1996). The former approach is based on the assumption that equal opportunities equates with 'equal access'. The 'special escalator' approach is clearly more active; it acknowledges that in order to promote equal access, special attention needs to be given to disadvantaged individuals and groups so that they can *compete* more effectively within society. This approach is underpinned by the liberal ideological position (Watts, 1996b), identified in the previous section, which emphasises individual change rather than change in social systems and structures. From this perspective it is clear that discrimination within the labour market could continue and indeed be perpetuated by 'special escalator' approaches. In contrast, the 'equal outcomes' approach emphasises social change: here the opportunity structure (including education, training and employment) is the focus of attention. The notion of 'equal outcomes' can of course be also contrasted with 'equal access'. In their study of the performance of ethnic minority trainees on government training programmes, Noon and Ogbonna (1998) identified that whilst there was reasonable evidence of equality of *access* there were striking differences between ethnic groups in terms of training *outcomes*. These differences were not only in terms of employment entry but also in terms of qualifications gained by the trainees.

The fourfold typology is as follows (Education Department, 1987):

1 *The unlocked door* A stated or implicit policy seeking to ensure the removal of any formal restrictions based on gender or race. Essentially passive in nature, such an orientation would not recognise any possibility of racism or sexism residing within either the formal or the informal (hidden) curriculum. (For those unfamiliar with this term, the 'hidden curriculum' refers to all those aspects of education or training not formally taught but implied through, for example, the way male/female roles are portrayed in the establishment, e.g. whether the food for parents' evenings is always distributed by girls, etc.). The interests and abilities of students or trainees are assumed to be beyond the (proper) influence of the institution.

2 *The open door* Besides removing formal restrictions, course organisation and classroom content, methods and assessment are all reviewed to remove any overt gender or racial bias. While interests and abilities are assumed to be beyond the influence of the school, college or training provider, these can seek to provide an unbiased experience for students or trainees.

3 *The special escalator* In addition to reforming access to, and the content of, courses, attention is paid to nurturing the knowledge, skills and attitudes of students or trainees to enable them to participate together in adult life. Besides a substantial common core to avoid forced choices, special 'compensatory' provision – in such forms as single sex or ethnic group (starter and bridging) courses – may be introduced. Education or training is seen as an opportunity to counter race or gender inequalities and stereotypes by developing the interests and abilities of students or trainees so they may compete and work together in adult life.

4 *Equal outcomes* Education and training are radically restructured with the aim of securing equitable take-up, qualification and subsequent achievement amongst gender and ethnic groups. There is an emphasis on identifying and setting targets for educational and training outcomes. Education and training are seen as a means of countering gender and racial inequalities and stereotypes by seeking to secure similar outcomes in education, training and employment.

An example of an 'equal outcomes' approach, which comes again from TVEI, can be found in the development of performance indicators for equal opportunities work. These performance indicators or statements of entitlement, which were intended to focus on *student outcomes*, are given in Table 7.1.

The statements of entitlement outlined in Table 7.1 were supported by a range of quantitative and qualitative evidence requirements. As an example, the evidence requirements for Entitlement 4 are given in Table 7.2.

The examples given in Tables 7.1 and 7.2 demonstrate that the translation of 'equal outcomes' principles into policy and practice is problematic. Not only is it difficult to measure 'outcomes' such as these, it is also difficult to ensure their *relevance*. As such, the 'equal outcomes' approach potentially oppresses its intended beneficiaries.

Returning to the fourfold typology, it should be emphasised that this is an artefact of 1980s equal opportunities discourse. As an artefact of its time the typology demonstrates that the concept of 'equal opportunities' has profound limitations, i.e. not only is there a problem of definition, but also the definitions that are in popular usage focus primarily on the *distribution* of resources. However, the once dominant discourse of equal opportunities has evolved into a present-day concern for social justice and social exclusion – a concern that goes beyond the politics of resource distribution. In the

Table 7.1 *Equal opportunities statements of entitlement*

1	That no category of student should be evidently underachieving
2	That categories of students under-represented in technology, science and modern language courses should be encouraged to take up those areas
3	That categories of students which are currently under-represented in higher education should be encouraged to progress to higher skill levels
4	That no single category of school leaver should feature disproportionately among the unemployed
5	That jobs should not be perceived as 'appropriate' for any single category of students
6	That all school leavers should be participating in further training

Source: TVEI Race and Gender Network, Employment Department, 1992

Table 7.2 *Evidence requirements for equal opportunities entitlement 4*

Entitlement 4
That no single category of school leaver should feature disproportionately among the unemployed

Quantitative data to be collected
Student destinations from institutions over a period of time

Qualitative evidence may be drawn from the following management strategies

Access courses, basic skills workshops, accreditation of prior learning

Education business partnerships

Liaison with parents and within the community

Compacts

Source: TVEI Race and Gender Network, Employment Department, 1992

following section various discourses of social justice and social exclusion will be explored as a preamble to considering a conceptual framework for anti-oppressive practice in career helping contexts.

Discourses of social justice and social exclusion

Griffiths has defined social justice as:

> a dynamic state of affairs which is good for the common interest, where that is taken to include the good of each other and also the good of all, in an acknowledgement that one depends on the other. The good depends on there being the right distribution of benefits and responsibilities. (1998: 302)

Underpinning this definition is an acknowledgement of the tension between the Enlightenment project which holds that human progress is possible, and the postmodernist view that any progress against oppression always carries with it the danger of constructing new forms of oppression. However, Griffiths suggests that by embracing this tension it is possible to construct a practical politics (Spivak, 1990) of 'pessimistic activism'. Griffiths defines this form of activism as a 'practical belief that even though there is no hope of final success the struggle is worthwhile anyway' (1998: 306).

More specifically, Fraser (1997) has identified two forms of social *injustice*: economic injustice and cultural injustice. The former involves exploitation, economic marginalisation and deprivation. The latter includes cultural domination, non-recognition and disrespect. According to Fraser, a dilemma of 'redistribution–recognition' is created when groups experience both economic *and* cultural injustices:

> redistributive remedies for political-economic injustice always dedifferentiate social groups; recognition remedies for cultural-valuational injustice always enhance social group differentiation. (1997: 23)

This dilemma can be related to the more familiar 'equality–difference' dichotomy which is concerned with the tension between promoting equality (which requires the use of essentialisms) and acknowledging individual difference (which seeks to challenge essentialisms). This serves to emphasise that the redistribution of resources is often achieved on the basis of assumed commonalities within and between groups. This in itself can be oppressive for those who do not identify with the commonalities that they are assumed to have with others. Furthermore, the very construction and application of commonalities as a basis for resource redistribution may be fundamentally oppressive, particularly if this is undertaken without the participation of the intended recipients. In this regard, Power and Gewirtz (1999) add to and augment Fraser's economic–cultural distinction by identifying a third category: *associational* injustice. Associational injustice is defined as:

patterns of association amongst individuals and amongst social groups which prevent some people from participating fully in decisions which affect the conditions within which they live and act. (1999: 4)

The distinction between economic, cultural and associational injustices can be usefully compared with Lister's (1999) analysis of the various contemporary discourses of social exclusion. Here Lister identifies three forms of discourse. The first is a *redistributive* discourse that relates to notions of citizenship and social rights. The second is an *individualistic* discourse which pathologises individuals and groups as a means of constructing the notion of 'the socially excluded'. The third is an *integrationist* discourse which gives primacy to 'paid work, supported by education and training, as the key route to social inclusion' (1999: 4).

As Power and Gewirtz (1999) suggest, when taken together the discourses of injustice and social exclusion outlined above provide a powerful conceptual framework for analysing social justice issues. For example, the Connexions strategy can be seen to be founded upon both an integrationist and an individualistic discourse. The discourse of individualism can be found in the construction of the 'disaffected' young person. Piper and Piper take issue with the term 'disaffected':

> 'Dissaffected youth' is a label with the potential to be superimposed across a range of widely variable situations, with inevitable implications for status and self concept, creating the necessary conditions for a negative career. It defines its recipient as pathological and further diminishes the power of the already disempowered. (1998: 35)

Thus, the construction of the category 'disaffected' can be seen as a form of *cultural* injustice, whereby subordinated groups of young people are stigmatised. It is important at this point to note some of the recent research which has acknowledged the positive cultural attributes of 'socially excluded' groups (Burghes and Brown, 1995; Webster, 2000). The term 'disaffected' also provides an example of the 'redistribution–recognition' dilemma. The Connexions strategy, at the time of writing, is premised on redirecting resources to those young people who are 'most at risk of encountering obstacles to a successful transition to adulthood' (DfEE, 2000c). However, as Piper and Piper (1998) suggest, by superimposing the category 'disaffected' on young people, social groups are dedifferentiated, thus leading to problems of recognition and valuation. Thus, the problem of recognition is not confined to those deemed to be 'disaffected'. Indeed, there is already a counter-lobby gathering momentum on behalf of 'non-disaffected' young people who feel excluded from career helping provision as a result of the redistribution of resources. It is here that the notion of associational injustice becomes significant.

The Connexions strategy is based upon eight declared principles, one of which relates to service user consultation. This is defined as:

> Taking account of the views of young people – individually and collectively, as the new service is developed and as it is operated locally. (DfEE, 2000c: 11)

Whilst there is some indication of the DfEE pursuing this principle in practice (DfEE, 2000e), a careful reading of the Connexions partnership bids will provide the first opportunity to assess the degree to which associational injustices are implicit in the design of service provision.

The foregoing has addressed the cultural and associational injustices that are implied by the individualistic discourse of the emerging Connexions strategy. In what follows, the integrationist discourse of Connexions will also be considered. The discourse of integrationism is clearly signposted by the following statement by Prime Minister Tony Blair:

> The best defence against social exclusion is having a job and the best way to get a job is to have a good education, with the right training and experience. (1999: 6)

This clearly identifies *paid* work, supported by education and training, as the principal pathway to social inclusion. However, this policy position does not address the *economic injustices* experienced by individuals and groups. Rather, an explicit integrationist stance combines here with an implicit individualism to locate the problem of exclusion in the pathology of the individual rather than in the structure of the labour market. Attention will now be given to ways in which the structure of the labour market maintains and reproduces economic injustices.

It is clear that people with multiple disadvantages continue to experience difficulties in accessing both the competitive labour market and government employment programmes (DFEE, 1999d). A key characteristic of the UK's labour market is its increased flexibility in comparison with its continental counterparts (Rajan et al., 1997). For example, it is estimated that 50 per cent of employers in the UK are using flexible forms of work. Under these conditions the relationship between employer and employee is redefined: employees are encouraged to perceive their employers as customers of their skills and services. As such, 'job security' is translated into 'employability', whereby employees forgo security for high-quality training which, in turn, provides them with the necessary transferable skills for survival and success in the competitive labour market. Employability has been defined as the ability to obtain and retain a job, and cope with the changes within the job (Rajan et al., 1999). It therefore places the responsibility firmly on the individual who, in order to be employable and competitive in the labour market, must develop and deploy career management skills.

Employability is also seen as a means of tackling long-term unemployment and social exclusion (Evans et al., 1999). It is the cornerstone of the current Labour government's Welfare to Work policy, of which the major initiative is the New Deal. As a government employment programme, the New Deal is unique in that it has been introduced at a time when employment is rising. As such, the New Deal is built upon the notion that the simple equilibrium model of the labour market does not work (Corrigan, 1997). Rather, there is an acknowledgement that the competitive labour market contributes to social exclusion through its recruitment practices. As Gordon (1997) has suggested, this is a cumulative process: those who are in a weak position in the labour market first become marginalised and subsequently excluded. However, by importing the notion of *employability* into the New Deal, the emphasis on open competition remains and, under these conditions, employers' expectations remain unchallenged. Further evidence of this claim will now be presented.

In general terms, the labour market can be categorised as follows:

1 Large national and multinational companies and substantial public sector organisations. Most will have considerable capacity within their human resource departments and many will have a corporate community involvement strategy.
2 Medium companies with 25–250 employees. Most will have a personnel and training section of limited capacity. Few will have a formal community involvement strategy.
3 Micro-enterprises with 1–5 employees, and small firms with up to 25 staff. There will be no formal personnel and training function. Investment in informal staff development may be evident. A formal community involvement strategy is unlikely.

Government employment programmes have traditionally drawn from categories 2 and 3. It is currently estimated that only 25 per cent of New Deal employers fall within category 1 (DfEE, 1999d). Within the competitive labour market the expectations of employers are clear and consistent. In a recent survey of 100 employers who regularly recruit non-graduates (Andersen Consulting, 1998), many indicated that they expected new entrants to be 'job-ready'. More than one-third specified 'communication and interpersonal skills' as the most important attribute; less than 10 per cent identified qualifications as being important. This trend has been replicated in a number of other recent studies (Employment Service, 1997; 1999; Public Attitude Surveys, 1997). This stress on social skills emphasises the need for employees to conform to social norms of behaviour and self-presentation which are strongly gender, ethnic and class specific. Furthermore, a DSS (1998) report found that employers were particularly concerned with the reasons given for long-term unemployment. Some explanations were not regarded sympathetically: these included disputes with former employers, criminal records and any indication of a lack of motivation not to live on state benefits.

The foregoing clearly indicates that government programmes such as New Deal are not designed to engage in *transformative* action, i.e. action designed to alleviate economic injustices through a restructuring of the labour market. By the same token, the individualistic and integrationist discourses that underpin the Connexions strategy would suggest that the new service would ultimately be poorly placed to address the economic injustices experienced by its primary client group. Once again, a careful reading of the Connexions partnership bids will provide the means to explore this question.

This section has been concerned with demonstrating the dilemmas and tensions that exist in any set of questions and actions that relate to social justice and social inclusion. It is the author's contention that, whilst there is no ultimate resolution to these dilemmas and tensions, nonetheless they need to be engaged with through ever evolving forms of anti-oppressive practice. The following section will present a conceptual framework for anti-oppressive practice drawing on the various perspectives discussed thus far.

A conceptual framework for anti-oppressive practice

The framework given in Figure 7.1 illustrates the various discourses of social justice and social inclusion outlined in the previous section. Each element of the framework will now be described.

The horizontal axis maps out two key concepts related to anti-oppressive practice: the concepts of *development need* and *advocacy*. Development need models of practice emphasise individual change: here career helpers work to help the individual *adapt* to social norms (e.g. employers' requirements, environmental conditions, cultural expectations etc.). It is informed by an *integrationist* discourse which focuses on individual development. In contrast, advocacy models of practice emphasise social change: here career

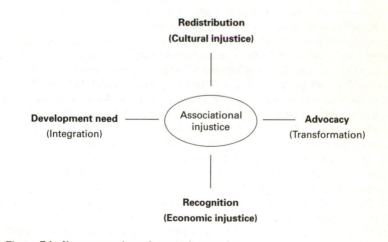

Figure 7.1 *Key concepts in anti-oppressive practice*

helpers work to modify and change the practice of institutions (employers, schools, training providers etc.). It is informed by a *transformative* discourse which focuses on restructuring socio-economic relations. Advocacy work could include challenging the selection criteria of opportunity providers, promoting the interests of a particular group of clients through networking and lobbying, and so on.

The vertical axis in Figure 7.1 maps out the tension between the *redistribution* of resources, which requires the construction and application of typifications,[1] and *recognition* which requires the deconstruction of typifications in favour of *difference*. The vertical axis also maps out the analytical distinction between *economic* and *cultural* injustices. This assumes that redistribution remedies are the primary means for countering economic injustice; as such there is potential for cultural injustice through *misrecognition*. This set of relationships can be explained as follows:

1 *Redistribution remedies* assume a degree of commonality of experience and identity amongst individuals and groups: this might be on the basis of gender, race, disability, sexuality etc. Contemporary examples include the perceived need to broaden the aspirations of young Muslim women. The disadvantages of this position are that typifications such as these may be oppressive to groups and individuals.
2 *Recognition remedies* seek to valorise individual experience and identity: this sits particularly well within a client-centred model of career helping which recognises and respects individual differences in terms of aspiration. Here aspirations are accepted on the basis of individual motives, needs, satisfactions etc. The disadvantage of this position is that such acceptance can deny the social influences that serve to constrain the individual's perception of what is possible. Furthermore, the differentiation of individuals and groups potentially disperses the power base upon which collective action might take place, and through which the redistribution of resources might be justified.

Finally, at the centre of the framework is the concept of *associational* injustice. Its location here serves to demonstrate that anti-oppressive practice should ensure that clients are *participants* rather than *recipients* of any action.

Thus, the framework given in Figure 7.1. presents four contrasting concepts: *redistribution, recognition, development need* and *advocacy*. Taken together, these concepts present any number of dilemmas and tensions. These might include the following examples: 'By recognising individual difference, am I mitigating against the potential redistribution of resources to groups and communities?'; 'In focusing on the development needs of individuals, am I in danger of reproducing oppressive labour market practices?'; 'If I advocate on behalf of a group, am I making assumptions based on typifications about individuals and groups?' These examples would suggest that anti-oppressive practice can be seen as a form of 'practical politics', the first rule being that there is no final solution, rather there are a set of questions that we can apply to the complex dynamics of day-to-day career helping practice.

In the final section of this chapter, consideration will be given to the sort of 'practical politics' that career helpers might undertake as a basis for anti-discriminatory practice.

A practical politics for anti-oppressive practice

This final section will begin by introducing a set of principles for day-to-day practice. The WISE principles given in Table 7.3 have clear implications for practitioners, the organisations within which they work, and the wider network within which both practitioners and organisations are located and interact. Taken together, the WISE principles and the conceptual framework given in the previous section provide a basis for a practical politics which engages with both the fundamental *and* the strategic questions that relate to anti-oppressive practice.

Following Thompson (1997) and Griffiths (1998), the author suggests that the development of a practical politics for anti-discriminatory practice is a *collective* task. This is clearly demonstrated in the WISE principles. As Griffiths (1998) has suggested, collective action can be most effective when participants are drawn from different backgrounds and perspectives. This does not mean that participants *represent* a particular constituency. Rather, it means that their backgrounds include constituencies who have *influenced* the perspectives that they hold.

Table 7.3 *The WISE principles for anti-oppressive practice*

Welcome Welcome diversity in society, and make welcome groups and individual people at risk of oppression, by appreciating their history and valuing their culture, identity, experience and contribution; respect individuality and avoid stereotyping.

Image Be aware of the damage that can be done, however unconsciously, by negative imagery (e.g. of danger, sickness, childlikeness, worthlessness, ridicule) in language, buildings, service structures, pictures, notices etc., and strive to replace them with positive, helpful imagery that reflects value, equality, respect, dignity and citizenship.

Support Offer support to enable people to function well in society; this may include interpreting for users of other languages, aids and equipment for disabled people, attention to access and presentation of materials, good information services, ensuring comfort and good health care, supporting networks of friendship or common interest etc.

Empowerment Support self-help and self-advocacy; listen to what people say and learn from them; involve people in decisions; give and support advocacy for people; ensure rights through entitlements and legislation; provide equal opportunities and practice anti-discrimination.

The four principles interact. You *welcome* people by surrounding them with positive imagery, offering them practical support and ensuring they are empowered; you provide a positive *image* of people by welcoming them, supporting them and empowering them; you *support* people by welcoming them, presenting positive images of them and empowering them; you *empower* people through welcome, positive imagery and practical support.

Career helpers have considerable potential for fostering collective action. This potential relates to their unique position as mediators between both individuals and groups, and the labour market. In undertaking their mediating role, career helpers work within a complex and comprehensive network. Network members include educational institutions, employers, training providers, voluntary organisations, government agencies etc. Clearly there is potential for an exponential increase in the value of this network at the point of collective action.

Finally, as Chapter 3 has indicated, the role of supervision is of critical importance in this context. The supervisory diad is by definition more than one person, and where more than one gather together a practical politics for anti-oppressive practice can emerge and be sustained.

Notes

The author would like to thank Morwenna Griffiths (Nottingham Trent University) and Paul Williams (The University of Reading) whose work has informed the writing of this chapter.

1 Thompson has defined a 'typification' as 'a set of characteristics and expectations we associate with a particular person, or group' (1997: 27). Thompson contrasts 'typifications', which he sees as having positive outcomes, with 'stereotypes' which are oppressive. This distinction is similar to the view held by Braidotti (1989) who suggests that 'essentialisms' are of critical importance to any project concerned with emancipation.

8

THE FUTURE OF CAREERS GUIDANCE

The many and far-reaching social, economic, political, cultural and technological changes that have occurred in the recent past have inevitably
influenced the direction in which careers guidance is moving. It is only
possible to speculate as to what the future holds, but there are a number of
well defined trends which indicate how careers guidance is likely to develop
in the next few years.

Information and communication technology

From originally being an interesting adjunct to guidance, the computer
and, more recently, the Internet have radically changed the 'map' of careers
guidance. Those working in the field now need to understand and utilise
the many applications of this new technology in their work. In doing so
they also need to construct a new and coherent model of guidance.
Watts (1996c) states that the computer offers both a major opportunity
of better quality careers guidance while also threatening to mechanise
the human dimension of the guidance process. The number of computer
assisted guidance systems (cags) has expanded greatly, partly due to the
Government seeing them as cutting the cost of guidance. The systems offer
a range of activities: self assessment, information retrieval, matching
jobs to individuals, decision aids and job seeking programmes. In future,
the task for practitioners will be to effectively integrate these systems
into guidance programmes. Computers are much better than careers
staff at providing clients with the information they need, so the guidance
practitioner will need to concentrate on two roles; providing counselling
support to clients and managing a range of guidance resources.

Offer and Sampson (1999) consider the important issue of the quality of
guidance provision via ICT. With the growth and increased access to ICT,
the questions of quality standards and how to protect consumers looms
large. Offer and Sampson raise the question of whether, for example, cags
are used on their own or supported by face to face guidance and come to
the conclusion that it is a matter of what level of intervention is appropriate

and for whom. Guidelines are being developed in the USA and with them, evaluation. However, Offer and Sampson stress the urgent need for self-diagnostic packages that will facilitate the effective use of guidance available on the Internet.

Offer and Watts (1997) have produced an interesting review of the Internet and careers work. The Web is now an important source of careers guidance. They set out its many uses, which include not just access to information via websites, but also direct access to cags. In addition, email counselling and video conferencing provides guidance at a distance to the individual or a group. There are exciting possibilities of reaching those who are isolated geographically or by disaffection. Electronic recruitment, placement and job search will continue to grow. The potential to deliver careers education via the Web is being exploited by universities, who are also using it to market their services. The increasing development of multimedia seems to be the next big step forward in the use of new technology in careers work. Widespread access to the new technology is crucial and those missing out are those who are disadvantaged already. Careers staff also need to be fully trained in using new systems.

Using ICT in careers guidance is part of the wider trend to utilise this technology in education. Tait (1999) points out that the assumptions about the boundary between cags and face to face guidance is constantly changing and needs to be continually re-assessed by practitioners. Watts (1996c) draws attention to the possibility of ICT moving careers guidance out of the control of the professionals and directly into the hands of the public; practitioners have to be aware of this and adapt accordingly.

The market and guidance

Since 1979, with the election of a 'New Right' government, the dominant political ideology has emphasised the central importance of market forces in British society. Allied to the notion of the market is a recognition of the desirability of competition, choice and the 'sovereignty' of the consumer. In the mid 1990s, local careers services were taken out of local authority control and transformed into hybrid companies who were expected to be more efficient and responsive to their clientele. Underlying this trend was an expectation that the 'taxpayer's money' would be better spent, reducing the demand on public spending. Commercial pressures were also apparent in careers services in higher education, with an increasing reliance on raising income from sources such as employers, in order to maintain their core activities. Indeed, staff in these services have had to develop new skills in bidding for external funding so that they can expand into new but necessary areas such as work experience for students and career management teaching. This trend is certain to continue, with careers services seeking partnerships with various agencies in order to meet the increasing demands on their limited resources. As a result, careers service managers and staff are acquiring new skills in marketing, networking and entrepreneurship.

Linked to these changes has been a growing requirement for careers services to be accountable for their performance to government and their clients. Quality assurance procedures are now common practice and clear standards apply to a range of activities including equal opportunities. Targets are set and funding will be linked to meeting these performance indicators, for example, the Final Destination Return of Graduates submitted each year by universities. The result of these trends means all careers services will be more accountable, having to meet demanding targets, needing to raise a greater proportion of their own funding and being required to work more closely with other partners.

Theory, research and practice

A number of authors have focused attention on the need for new theoretical frameworks to explain career development and appropriate guidance in the new era (Collin and Watts l996; Law 1996, 1999; Savickas 1993). Collin (1997) goes further than this when she suggests there is need for a much closer relationship between those engaged in research, theory building, and practice because they are all engaged, with clients, in constructing meaning.

There has been much theorising about the nature of the new era, and much of this is relevant to understanding the context in which careers guidance is located. For example, Beck describes life in a 'runaway world'. in this world, the emphasis is upon self fulfilment and achievement with people required to take their lives into their own hands, with individuals becoming 'actors, builders, jugglers and stage managers of their own biographies and identities' (2000: 166). In a climate of insecurity, individual blame and responsibility is stressed. Life events are now attributed to external events such as structural unemployment, not to the individual. Beck also refers to the globalisation of biography, with individuals increasingly living transnational lives, with hybrid identities and cultures. Lives therefore become experimental because there are no historical models or recipes for living. Social reflection and active management become necessary. Life is constructed out of a process of testing several overlapping identities.

Arthur et al. (1999) maintain that existing career theories 'don't highlight how people can enact their own careers, in their own frameworks, and in the process contribute to, rather than simply respond to, the unfolding New Economy' (1999: 63). Their research showed that typically the people they talked to had had three different employers over a ten year period, with most moves voluntary. They refer to the work of Weick (1996) who describes how people enact their careers and the environment in which careers take place. In so doing, they create their own career narratives as a means of personal sense making. They don't plan their careers, so much as improvise. The apparent discontinuity in modern careers can be seen as a virtue, giving the opportunity for learning. The old objective view of career as continuous is being replaced by a more subjective and personal experience which has meaning to the individual. What becomes important is three areas of career competency: the knowing why meaning derived from the individual career; the knowing how skills and job knowledge accumulated and the knowing-whom relationships that have developed. The three can be seen as career capital.

Arthur et al. (1999) predict that flexibility, versatility, improvisation and persistent learning will increasingly determine personal survival and growth, and that work will be seen as a series of experiments. They observe that women are more likely to have a more flexible pattern of response than men. This largely optimistic account of the 'new careers' needs to be considered in the light of different assessments of contemporary work patterns.

For example, Burchell et al. (1999) indicate high levels of insecurity at work, as well as an increased pace of work. Fear of redundancy was less than a loss of valued job features such as promotion, and there was a clear divide between workforce and management. Job insecurity led to deteriorating physical and mental well being and increased tension at home. Sonnenberg (1997) examined how 'new career' leads to increasing anxiety in the workplace and how those involved in workplace counselling and careers guidance need a special awareness of this and the ability to 'contain' their clients, who are also likely to be experiencing personal developmental issues as well. He stresses the importance of supervision for those engaged in these demanding professions.

Research and theory in career development has tended to ignore large numbers of people according to Fitzgerald and Betz (1994). They describe how the role of gender, race, class and sexual orientation has been overlooked by career theorists. The need to consider the changing experiences of women who increasingly have to balance career and relationships is acknowledged by Kaltreider et al. (1997), in exploring the dilemmas of a 'double life'. A clearer understanding of life span development and the experience of transitions is necessary in order to understand the life experiences of the wider variety of clients now seeking careers guidance (Gothard 1996; Seligman, 1994; Sugarman, 1996).

The implications for careers guidance and counselling in the postmodern era is explored by Collin (1997), Collin and Watts (1996) and Savickas (1993), with very similar conclusions. There is agreement that careers guidance should be part of a wider process, potentially linked to financial guidance, relationship counselling and stress counselling, thus addressing the needs of the whole person, and recognising 'the distinction between personal and career counselling as a wall created by words' (Savickas 1993: 211). As regards appropriate theory, constructivist approaches are favoured as they emphasise the need to help clients narrate a coherent, continuous and credible story (Collin and Watts 1996). This is in contrast to the traditional approach of trying to fit the client to a job; in future, the emphasis should be on enabling the client to manage his or her career by developing a range of appropriate skills around life long learning. Careers workers should be less experts and more 'cultural workers who seek to remove barriers that keep people from speaking for themselves' (Savickas 1993: 210–11). Savickas also emphasises the multicultural diversity of clients and the need for career counsellors to recognise the individuality of their clients which can best be understood through their life stories rather than by traditional means of assessing clients using psychometric tools. The supposed certainty of such objective measures is likely to be replaced by an approach that acknowledges uncertainty and explores with the client, as co-author, the meaning and purpose lying behind their autobiography.

In future, there is certainly a need for career researchers and theorists to make their work more relevant and accessible to practitioners and this is evident in texts using case studies as a means of relating theory to practice (Brown and Brooks, 1996, Swanson and Fouad, 1999). Another approach is to show the relationship between career development theory and models of guidance (Gothard and Mignot, 1999), so that practitioners can see more easily the relevance of theory to their work.

A new professional identity?

Careers guidance has become explicitly drawn onto the agenda of recent governments because of the increasing importance attached to the employability of young people. New Labour have made this a priority and put emphasis on the role of careers guidance in tackling the issue of social exclusion. This has led to an important new development, the creation of a youth support service, Connexions, which for the first time, will break down the professional barriers between helping agencies. The service will change the focus of careers guidance away from its original mission of providing careers advice to all young people, and the priority will be given to those aged 13 to 19 who are most at risk.

The introduction of the Connexions Service seems likely to herald the most radical change in the careers guidance profession. At the same time, a new framework for training, the Qualification in Careers Guidance (QCG) is being piloted and will replace the existing framework in 2002. Both of these developments need to be considered in order to understand the future professional identity of careers staff. The new personal adviser role, which will be central in Connexions, involves giving information, advice and guidance to young people aged 13 to 19 on education, career, health, social welfare and youth justice issues. The emphasis will be on brokering, a skill not referred to previously in the role of careers staff, although possibly implicit in the networking and referral skills set out in the QCG. A recent survey of careers company staff (DfEE, 2000b) indicated considerable concern about the acquisition of new skills required by Connexions.

It is clear from both developments, that equal opportunities will be at the forefront of careers guidance work in the future. The personal adviser will be expected to challenge stereotypes; while the ethnic mix of the Careers Service (DfEE, 2000b) will need to be more representative of the communities they serve, particularly at management level. The QCG's emphasis on core values, self evaluation and equal opportunities puts an onus on newly trained careers staff to become the reflective practitioner Schon (1991) recommends.

At the time of writing there is still a lot of uncertainty about how Connexions will operate and in particular, how personal advisers will be trained. However, it is clear that the existing roles of careers workers will be subsumed into new roles which differ significantly. Personal advisers will have a much wider role working more intensively with young people who have real difficulties. New skills, knowledge and understanding will be required, making the role an especially demanding one. It is a role with plenty of potential conflicts in terms of having to meet tough targets and yet having to be client centred. There is a real danger that careers guidance will lose its particular professional identity in Connexions, and there are well founded fears that careers work will suffer accordingly.

Careers guidance is changing with the times and this inevitably raises a number of important questions. Will the profession continue to exist within the new Connexions service or will it become just an important part of a more holistic service? Will ICT increasingly deliver careers guidance at the expense of traditional personal guidance? Will the emphasis on helping young people at risk draw attention away from the need for life long guidance? Can careers services continue to be increasingly commercial and still serve all clients equitably? The need for high quality careers guidance has never been greater; the challenge remains of how best to provide it to all those clients who require it.

REFERENCES

Adnett, N. (1989) *Labour Market Policy*. Harlow: Longman.

ADSET (1995) *Local Labour Market Information: a National Quality Assurance Framework*. Kettering: Association for Database Services in Education and Training.

Ali, L. and Graham, B. (1996) *The Counselling Approach to Careers Guidance*. London: Routledge.

Andersen Consulting (1998) *The Attributes of Youth – Young People, Education and Employability*. London: Andersen Consulting.

Arnold, J. and Jackson, C. (1997) 'The new career: issues and challenges', *British Journal of Guidance and Counselling*, 25 (4): 427–33.

Arthur, M.B., Inkson, K. and Pringle, J.K. (1999) *The New Careers*. London: Individual Action.

Astin, H. (1984) 'The meaning of work in women's lives', *Counselling Psychologist*, 12 (4): 117–33.

Atkinson, J. (1985) *The Changing Corporation*. Sussex: Institute of Manpower Studies.

BAC (1988) *Code of Ethics and Practice for the Supervision of Counsellors*. Rugby: British Association of Counsellors.

Barglow, R. (1994) *The Crisis of the Self in the Age of Information*. London: Routledge.

Barnes, A. and Andrews, D. (1995) *Developing Careers Education and Guidance in the Curriculum*. London: David Fulton.

Basit, T. (1996) 'I'd hate to be just a housewife: career aspirations of British Muslim girls', *British Journal of Guidance and Counselling*, 24 (2): 227–42.

Bates, I. (1984) 'From vocational guidance to life skills: historical perspectives on careers education', in I. Bates, J. Clarke, P. Cohen, D. Finn, R. Moore and P. Willis (eds) *Schooling for the Dole? The New Vocationalism*. London: Macmillan.

Bates, I. (1998) 'The politics of careers education and guidance: a case for scrutiny', in R. Edwards, R. Harrison and A. Tait (eds), *Telling Tales: Perspectives on Guidance and Counselling in Learning*. London, Routledge.

Bayliss, V. (1998) *Redefining Work*. London: Royal Society of Arts.

Beck, U. (1999) *World Risk Society*. Cambridge: Polity.

Bedford, T. (1982) *Vocational Guidance Interviews*. London: Department of Employment.

Bentley, T. and Gurumurthy, R. (1999) *Destinations Unknown*. London: Demos.

Bimrose, J. (1993) 'Counselling and social context', in R. Bayne and P. Nicolson (eds), *Counselling and Psychology for Health Professionals*. London: Chapman & Hall. pp. 149–65.

Blair, T. (1999) 'Foreword' to *Bridging the Gap: New Opportunities for 16–18 Year Olds Not in Education, Training or Employment*. Social Exclusion Unit. London: Stationery Office.

Bradley, H., Erickson, M., Stephenson, C. and Williams, S. (2000) *Myths at Work*. Cambridge: Polity.

Braidotti, R. (1989) 'The politics of ontological difference', in T. Brennan (ed.), *Between Feminism and Psychoanalysis*. London: Routledge.

Brammer, L. (1985) *The Helping Relationship*. Englewood Cliffs, NJ: Prentice-Hall.

Brockett, R.G. and Hiemstra, R. (1991) *Self-Direction in Adult Learning: Perspectives on Theory, Research and Practice*. London: Routledge.

Brown, A. (1997) 'Time for a change (of rhetoric): the implications of changing patterns of careers for guidance practice', paper presented at a conference on The Effective Use of LMI in Careers Guidance and Careers Education, University of Warwick, Institute of Employment Research.

Brown, D. (1996) 'The status of career development theories', in D. Brown and L. Brooks (eds), *Career Choice and Development*, 3rd edn. San Francisco, CA: Jossey-Bass. pp. 513–25.

Brown, D. and Brooks, L. (1996) *Career Choice and Development*, 3rd edn. San Francisco, CA: Jossey-Bass.

Burchell, B.J., Day, D., Hudson, M., Ladipe, D., Mankelow, R., Nolan, J.P., Reed, H., Wichert, I.C. and Wilkinson, F. (1999) *Job Insecurity and Work Intensification: Flexibility and the Changing Boundaries of Work*. York: YPS.

Burghes, L. and Brown, M. (1995) *Single Lone Mothers: Problems, Prospects and Policies*. York: Joseph Rowntree Foundation.

Bynner, J., Ferri, E. and Stapleford, P. (1997) *Twenty Something in the 1990s*. Aldershot: Ashgate.

Bysshe, S., Berry-Lound, D., Ball, B., Bufton, B. and Mulvey, R. (1997) *Group Work: A Review and Evaluative Study of Careers Service Provision in Years 9, 10 and 11*. Suffolk: DfEE Publications.

Campbell, J. (1998) *The Inner Reaches of Outer Space: Metaphor as Myth and as Religion*. New York: Van Der Marck.

Carifio, M.S. and Hess, A.K. (1987) 'Who is the ideal supervisor?', *Professional Psychology: Research and Practice*, 18: 244–50.

Castells, M. (1999a) *The Rise of the Network Society*. Oxford: Blackwell.

Castells, M. (1999b) *The Power of Identity*. Oxford: Blackwell.

CBI (1989) *Towards a Skills Revolution*. London: Confederation of British Industry.

CBI (1993a) *Routes for Success: Careership. A Strategy for All 16–19-Year-Old Learning*. London: Confederation of British Industry.

CBI (1993b) *A Credit to Your Career*. London: Confederation of British Industry.

Chen, P. (1997) 'Career projection: narrative in context', *Journal of Vocational Education and Training*, 49 (2): 311–26.

Clarke, H. (1994) 'What are careers officers thinking of? How information cues are selected and used in interviews', *British Journal of Guidance and Counselling*, 22 (2): 247–59.

Cochran, L. (1997) *Career Counselling: a Narrative Approach*. London: Sage.

Collin, A. (1996) 'Changes in the concept of "Career"', *NICEC Bulletin*, 46: 13–18.

Collin. A. (1997) 'Career in context', *British Journal of Guidance and Counselling*, 25 (4): 435–46.

Collin, A. and Watts, A. (1996) 'The death and transfiguration of career and career guidance', *British Journal of Guidance and Counselling*, 24 (3): 385–98.

Collin, A. and Young, R.A. (1986) 'New directions for theories of career', *Human Relations*, 39 (9): 837–53.

Collin, A. and Young, R.A. (1988) 'Career development and hermeneutical research', *Canadian Journal of Counselling*, 22 (4): 191–201.

Cormier, W.H. and Cormier, L.S. (1991) *Interviewing Strategies for Helpers*, 3rd edn. Pacific Grove, CA: Brooks/Cole.

Corrigan, P. (1997) 'The welfare to work programme', in *Exclusion, the New Deal and Welfare to Work*. London: Vision for London.

CRE (1992) *Psychometric Tests and Racial Equality*. London: Commission for Racial Equality.

CTAD (1996) *LMI Matters*. Cambridge: Cambridge Training and Development.

Davis, J. (1998) 'The threat of globalism', *Race and Class*, 40 (2/3): 37–48. London: Institute of Race Relations.

Dawis, R. (1996) 'Theory of work adjustment and person–environment correspondence counselling', in D. Brown and L. Brooks (eds), *Career Choice and Development*, 3rd edn. San Francisco, CA: Jossey-Bass.

Daws, P. (1977) 'Are career education programmes in secondary schools a waste of time?', *British Journal of Guidance and Counselling*, 5 (1): 10–18.

DES/DE (1987) *Working Together for a Better Future*. Department for Education and Science and Department of Employment. London: HMSO.

DfEE (1995) *Competitiveness: Forging Ahead*. Department for Education and Employment. London: HMSO.

DfEE (1996) *Guidelines to Good Practice in Promoting Equal Opportunities in the Careers Service*. Sheffield: Department for Education and Employment.

DfEE (1997a) *Excellence in Schools*. Department for Education and Employment. London: HMSO.

DfEE (1997b) *Education Act*. Department for Education and Employment. London: HMSO.

DfEE (1997c) *Careers Education and Guidance in Schools*. Department for Education and Employment. London: HMSO.

DfEE (1998a) *Talking about 'Careers': Young People's Views of Careers Education and Guidance in School*. Sudbury: Department for Education and Employment.

DfEE (1998b) *Careers Service Planning Guidance*. Nottingham: Department for Education and Employment.

DfEE (1999a) *Better Choices: Developing the Careers Education Curriculum in Schools*. Nottingham: Department for Education and Employment.

DfEE (1999b) *Careers Service Planning Guidance*. Nottingham: Department for Education and Employment.

DfEE (1999c) *The Careers Service and Young Muslim Women*. Nottingham: Department for Education and Employment.

DfEE (1999d) *Lasting Value: Recommendations for Increasing Retention within the New Deal*. Sheffield: New Deal Task Force Working Group on Retention.

DfEE (1999e) *The Learning Age. Local Information, Advice and Guidance for Adults in England: towards a National Framework*. London: Department for Education and Employment.

DfEE (2000a) *Connexions: the Best Start in Life for Every Young Person*. Nottingham: Department for Education and Employment.

DfEE (2000b) *1999 Survey of Careers Service*. Sudbury: Department for Education and Employment.

DfEE (2000c) *The Connexions Service: Prospectus and Specification*. Nottingham: Department for Education and Employment.

DfEE (2000d) *Research to Inform the Development of the Connexions Service. Conference report*. London: Department of Education and Employment.

DfEE (2000e) *A Review of Approaches to Involving Young People in a Public Service: Draft Report*. Sheffield: Department for Education and Employment.

DfEE (2000f) *Career-Related Learning in Primary Schools*. London: Department for Education and Employment.

DfEE/QCA (2000a) *Framework for Personal, Social and Health Education*. London: Department for Education and Employment/Qualifications and Curriculum Authority.

DfEE/QCA (2000b) *The National Curriculum: Handbook for Secondary Teachers in England*. London: Department for Education and Employment/Qualifications and Curriculum Authority.

DfEE/QCA (2000c) *Citizenship in Key Stages 3 and 4*. London: Department for Education and Employment/Qualifications and Curriculum Authority.

DSS (1998) *Recruiting Long-Term Unemployed People*. London: Department of Social Security.

DTI (1994) *Competitiveness: Helping Business to Win*. Department of Trade and Industry. London: HMSO.

Edwards, R. (1997) *Changing Places: Flexibility, Lifelong Learning and a Learning Society*. London: Routledge.

Edwards, R. and Payne, J. (1997) 'The self in guidance: assumptions and challenges', *British Journal of Guidance and Counselling*, 25 (4): 527–38.

Edwards, R., Raggatt, P., Harrison, R., McCollum, A. and Calder, J. (1998) *Recent Thinking in Lifelong Learning: a Review of the Literature*. Sudbury: Department for Education and Employment.

Edwards, T. (1997) 'Sexuality', in J. Roche and S. Tucker (eds), *Youth in Society*. London: Sage.

Egan, G. (1994) *The Skilled Helper: a Problem Management Approach to Helping*, 5th edn. Pacific Grove, CA: Brooks/Cole.

Employment Department (1987) *TVEI Developments 2: Equal Opportunities*. Sheffield: Employment Department.

Employment Department (1992) *Equal Opportunities Performance Indicators/ Statements of Entitlement*. Sheffield: Employment Department.

Employment Service (1997) *Increasing Employability: an Operational Perspective*. London: Employment Service.

Employment Service (1999) *New Deal for Young Unemployed People: a Good Deal for Employers?* London: Employment Service.

EOC (1999) *Research Discussion Series: Gender Equality and the Careers Service*. Manchester: Equal Opportunities Commission.

Erikson, E. (1968) *Identity, Youth and Crisis*. London: Faber.

Evans, C., Nathan, M. and Simmonds, D. (1999) *Employability Through Work*. Manchester: Centre for Local Economic Strategies.

Fevre, R. (1992) *The Sociology of Labour Markets*. Hemel Hempstead: Harvester Wheatsheaf.

Fitzgerald, L.F. and Betz, N.E. (1994) 'Career development in a cultural context: the role of gender, race, class, and sexual orientation', in M.L. Savickas and R.W. Lent (eds), *Convergence in Career Development Theories: Implications for Science and Practice*. Palo Alto, CA: Consulting Psychologists Press. pp. 103–17.

Fransella, F. and Dalton, P. (1990) *Personal Construct Counselling in Action*. London: Sage.

Fraser, N. (1997) *Justice Interruptus: Critical Reflections on the 'Postsocialist' Condition* London: Routledge.

Freire, P. (1973) *Pedagogy of the Oppressed*. New York: Seabury.

Gelatt, H.B. (1989) 'Positive uncertainty: a new decision-making framework for counseling', *Journal of Counseling Psychology*, 36(2): 252–6.

Giddens, A. (1994) *Modernity and Self Identity*. London: Polity.

Giddens, A. (2000) 'In Conversation' in W. Hutton and A. Giddens (eds), *On the Edge: Living with Global Capitalism*. London: Jonathan Cape.

Ginzberg, E. (1972) 'Towards a theory of occupational choice: a restatement', *Vocational Guidance Quarterly*, 20 (3): 169–76.

Goncalves, O.F. (1995) 'Hermeneutics, constructivism, and cognitive-behavioural therapies: from the object to the project', in R.A. Neimeyer and M.J. Mahony (eds), *Constructivism in Psychotherapy*. Washington: American Psychological Association.

Goodson, I. (1988) *The Making of the Curriculum*. Brighton: Falmer.

Gordon, I. (1997) 'Unemployment and labour exclusion in London', in *Exclusion, the New Deal and Welfare to Work*. London: Vision for London.

Gothard, B. (1996) 'The mid-life transition and career counselling in Britain', *Journal of Career Development*, 23 (2): 167–74.

Gothard, B. (1999) 'Career as myth', *Psychodynamic Counselling*, 5 (1): 87–97.

Gothard, B. and Mignot, P. (1999) 'Career counselling for the 21st century: integrating theory and practice', *The International Journal for the Advancement of Counselling*, 21: 153–67.

Gottfredson, L. (1981) 'Circumscription and compromise', *Journal of Counselling Psychology*, 28 (6): 545–79.

Gottfredson, L. (1996) 'Gottfredson's theory of circumscription', in D. Brown and L. Brooks (eds), *Career Choice and Development*, 3rd edn. San Francisco, CA: Jossey-Bass.

Griffiths, M. (1998) 'The discourses of social justice in schools', *British Educational Research Journal*, 24 (3): 301–5.

Hage, J. and Powers, C. (1992) *Post Industrial Lives: Roles and Relationships in the 21st Century*. London: Sage.

Halmos, P. (1974) 'The personal and the political', *British Journal of Guidance and Counselling*, 2 (2): 130–48.

Handy, C. (1989) *Age of Unreason*. London: Hutchinson.

Harris, S. (1999) *Careers Education: Contesting Policy and Practice*. London: Paul Chapman.

Hawkins, P. (1997) *Skills for Graduates in the 21st Century in Decision Making for Life Long Learning*. Brussels: VUB Press.

Hawkins, P. and Shohet, R. (1989) *Supervision in the Helping Professions*. Milton Keynes: Open University Press.

Hawkins, P. and Winter, J. (1997) *Mastering Change: Learning the Lessons of the Enterprise in Higher Education Initiative*. Sheffield: DfEE.

Hess, A.K. (ed.) (1980) *Psychotherapy Supervision: Theory, Research and Practice*. New York: Wiley.

Higgins, R. and Westergaard, J. (1998) 'In search of guidance models for the group context', in *Occasional Papers in Careers Guidance No. 2: a Collection of Professional Papers by Staff of the College of Guidance Studies*. Stourbridge: Institute of Careers Guidance.

Hillage, J. and Pollard, E. (1998) *Employability: Developing a Framework for Policy Analysis*. DfEE Research Series RR85. London: DfEE.

Hirsh, W., Kidd, J.M. and Watts, A.G. (1998) *Constructs of Work Used in Guidance*. Cambridge: CRAC.

Hobsbawm, E. (2000) *The New Century*. London: Little Brown.

Hodkinson, P., Sparkes, A.C. and Hodkinson, H. (1996) *Triumphs and Tears: Young People, Markets and the Transition from School to Work*. London: David Fulton.

Holland, J. (1973) *Making Vocational Choices*. Englewood Cliffs, NJ: Prentice-Hall.

Honey, P. and Mumford, A. (1982) *The Manual of Learning Styles*. Berks: Peter Honey.

Hughes, D. (2000) *Careers Service Work with Young People with Priority Needs: Examples of Practice*. Derby: Centre for Guidance Studies.

Hughes, D. and Morgan, S. (2000) *Research to Inform the Development of the New Connexions Service*. London: DfEE.

Hustler, D., Ball, B., Carter, K., Halsall, R., Ward, R. and Watts, A. (1998) *Developing Career Management Skills in Higher Education*. Cambridge: CRAC.

Ivey, A., Ivey, M. and Simek-Downing, L. (1987) *Counselling and Psychotherapy*, 2nd edn. Englewood Cliffs, NJ: Prentice-Hall.

Johnson, D.W. and Johnson, F.P. (1987) *Joining Together*. Englewood Cliffs, NJ: Prentice-Hall.

Jones, J.E. and Pfeiffer, J.W. (1980) *User's Guide to the Structured Experience Kit*. San Diego, CA: University Associates.

Juch, A. (1983) *Personal Development: Theory and Practice in Management Training*. Chichester: Shell International, Wiley.

Kaltreider, N.B. (1997) in N.B. Kaltreider (ed.), *Dilemmas of a Double Life: Women Balancing Careers and Relationships*. New Jersey: Northvale.

Karasu, T. (1984) *The Psychological Therapies*. Washington, DC: American Psychiatric Press.

Kelly, G.A. (1955) *The Psychology of Personal Constructs*, Vols 1 and 2. New York: Norton.

Kelly, G.A. (1991) *The Psychology of Personal Constructs*, Vols I and II. New York: Norton. Reprinted London: Routledge.

Kidd, J.M. (1996a) 'Career planning within work organisations', in A.G. Watts, B. Law, J. Killeen, J. Kidd and R. Hawthorn (eds), *Rethinking Careers Education and Guidance: Theory, Policy, and Practice*. London: Routledge.

Kidd, J.M. (1996b) 'The career counselling interview', in A.G. Watts, B. Law, J. Killeen, J. Kidd and R. Hawthorn (eds), *Rethinking Careers Education and Guidance: Theory, Policy, and Practice*. London: Routledge.

Kidd, J.M., Killeen, J., Jarvis, J. and Offer, M. (1994) 'Is guidance an applied science?', *British Journal of Guidance and Counselling*, 22 (3): 385–403.

Kidd, J.M., Killeen, J., Jarvis, J. and Offer, M. (1996) 'Competing schools or stylistic variations in careers guidance interviewing', *British Journal of Guidance and Counselling*, 25 (1): 47–66.

Killeen, J. (1996) 'The social context of guidance', in A.G. Watts, B. Law, J. Killeen, J. Kidd and R. Hawthorn (eds), *Rethinking Careers Education and Guidance: Theory, Policy, and Practice*. London: Routledge.

Killeen, J., White, M. and Watts, A.G. (1992) *The Economic Value of Careers Guidance*. London: Policy Studies Institute.

Knowles, M.S. (1983) 'Andragogy: an emerging technology for adult learning', in R. Edwards, A. Hanson and P. Raggatt (eds), *Boundaries of Adult Learning* (1996). London: Routledge and the Open University.

Knowles, M.S. (1984) *Andragogy in Action*. San Francisco/London: Jossey-Bass.

Kolb, D.A. (1984) *Experiential Learning: Experience as the Source of Learning and Development*. Englewood Cliffs, NJ: Prentice-Hall.

Kolb, D.A. (1985) *Learning Style Inventory*. Boston, MA: McBer.

Kolb, D.A. and Fry, R. (1975) 'Towards an applied theory of experiential learning', in D.A. Kolb and R. Fry (eds), *Theories of Group Process*. New York: Massachusetts Institute of Technology.

Kundnani, A. (1998) 'The rise of information capitalism', *Race and Class*, 40 (2/3): 49–72. London: Institute of Race Relations.

Lago, C. and Thompson, J. (1996) *Race, Culture and Counselling*. Buckingham: Open University Press.

Law, B. (1981) 'Community interaction: a "mid range" focus for theories of career development in young adults', *British Journal of Guidance and Counselling*, 9 (2): 142–58.

Law, B. (1984) 'Preface' to S. Kushner and T. Logan, *Made in England*. London: CARE.

Law, B. (1996a) 'A career learning theory', in A.G. Watts, B. Law, J. Killeen, J. Kidd and R. Hawthorn (eds), *Rethinking Careers Education and Guidance: Theory, Policy, and Practice*. London: Routledge.

Law, B. (1996b) 'Careers work in schools', in A.G. Watts, B. Law, J. Killeen, J. Kidd and R. Hawthorn (eds), *Rethinking Careers Education and Guidance: Theory, Policy, and Practice*. London: Routledge.

Law, B. (1996c) 'Careers education in the curriculum', in A.G. Watts, B. Law, J. Killeen, J. Kidd and R. Hawthorn (eds), *Rethinking Careers Education and Guidance: Theory, Policy, and Practice*. London: Routledge. pp. 216–32.

Law, B. (1999) 'Career learning space: a new DOTS thinking for careers education', *British Journal of Guidance and Counselling*, 27 (1): 23–34.

Law, B. (2000), 'Careers work policy: from alpha to omega', *Careers Adviser*, 4 (2): 4–8. London: Independent Educational Publishing.

Law, B. and McGowan, B. (1999) *Opening Doors*. Cambridge: CRAC.

Law, B. and Watts, A.G. (1977) *Schools, Careers and Community*. London: Church Information Office.

Levinson, D. (1996) *The Seasons of a Woman's Life*. New York: Knopf.

Levinson, D., Darrow, D., Klein, E., Levinson, M. and McKee, B. (1978) *The Seasons of a Man's Life*. New York: Knopf.

Levitas, R. (1998) *The Inclusive Society? Social Exclusion and New Labour*. London: Macmillan.

Lipsey, R.G. (1989) *An Introduction to Positive Economics*. London: Weidenfeld & Nicholson.

Lister, R. (1999) '"Work for those who can, security for those who cannot": a third way in social security reform?', paper presented to Social Policy Association Annual Conference, Roehampton Institute, London, July.

Maher, B.A. (ed.) (1969) *Clinical Psychology and Personality: the Selected Papers of George Kelly*. New York: Wiley.

Mair, M. (1989) 'Kelly, Bannister, and a story-telling psychology', *International Journal of Personal Construct Psychology*, 2: 1–14.

May, R. (1993) *The Cry for Myth*. London: Souvenir.

McChesney, P. (1995) 'Yes but how? Development and evaluation of careers education', *British Journal of Guidance and Counselling*, 23 (3): 327–45.

McLeod, J. (1996) 'The emerging narrative approach to counselling and psychotherapy', *British Journal of Guidance and Counselling*, 24 (2): 173–84.

Meijers, F. (1997) *Career Identity as a Form of Empowerment in Decision Making for Life Long Learning*. Brussels: VUB Press.

Mignot, P. (2000a) 'Using Visual Methods in Careers Education and Guidance', *Pastoral Care in Education*, June: 8–16.

Mignot, P. (2000b) 'Metaphor: a paradigm for practice-based research into "career"', *British Journal of Guidance and Counselling*, 28 (4): 515–31.

Mitchell, A., Jones, G. and Krumboltz, J. (1979) *Social Learning and Career Decision Making*. Rhode Island: Carroll.

Mitchell, L.K. and Krumboltz, J. (1996) 'Krumboltz's learning theory of career choice and counselling', in D. Brown and L. Brooks (eds), *Career Choice and Development*, 3rd edn. San Francisco: Jossey-Bass.

Morris, M., Rudd, P., Nelson, J. and Davies, D. (2000) *The Contribution of Careers Education and Guidance to School Effectiveness in 'Partnership' Schools*. Nottingham: NFER/DfEE.

Mulgan, G. (1997) *Connexity*. London: Chatto & Windus.

NACGT (1989) *Survey of Careers Education and Guidance in British Schools*. Stourbridge: NACGT.

NACGT (1999) *Survey of Careers Education and Guidance in British Schools*. Stourbridge: NACGT.

NACGT (2000) 'Reading guide of key publications to support policy and practice in CEG', revised May 2000. Stourbridge: NACGT.

NACGT/ICG (1993) *Careers Education and Guidance in British Schools*. Stourbridge: NACGT/ICG.

NACGT/ICG (1996) *Careers Education and Guidance in British Schools*. Stourbridge: NACGT/ICG.

National Commission of Inquiry into Higher Education (1997) *Higher Education in the Learning Society* (The Dearing Report). London: NCIHE.

NCC (1991) *Curriculum Guidance 6: Careers Education and Guidance*. York: National Curriculum Council.

Neimeyer, G.J. (1992) 'Personal constructs in career counselling and development', *Journal of Career Development*, 18 (3): 163–73.

Noon, M. and Ogbonna, E. (1998) 'Unequal provision? Ethnic minorities and employment training policy', *Journal of Education and Work*, 11 (1): 23–39.

NYA/DfEE (2000) *Engaging Young People in Planning, Management, Delivery and Evaluation of the Connexions Service*. London: National Youth Agency/DfEE.

Offer, M. and Sampson, J.P. (1999) 'Quality in the content and use of information and communications technology in guidance', *British Journal of Guidance and Counselling*, 27 (4): 501–16.

Offer, M. and Watts, A. (1997) *The Internet and Careers Work*. Cambridge: NICEC.

OFSTED (1995) *A Survey of Careers Education and Guidance in Schools*. London: HMSO.

OFSTED (1998a) *National Survey of Careers Education and Guidance: Secondary Schools*. London: OFSTED/DfEE.

OFSTED (1998b) *National Survey of Careers Education and Guidance: Special Schools and Pupil Referral Units*. London: OFSTED/DfEE.

OFSTED (1998c) *Work-Related Aspects of the Curriculum in Secondary Schools*. London: OFSTED.

OFSTED (1999) *Inspecting Schools: the Framework*. London: OFSTED.

OFSTED/Audit Commission (1992) *Unfinished Business*. Coventry: OFSTED/FEFC.

Osipow, S. (1983) *Theories of Career Development*. Englewood Cliffs, NJ: Prentice-Hall.

Parsons, F. (1909) *Choosing a Vocation*. Boston: Houghton Mifflin.

Payne, J. and Edwards, R. (1996) *Impartiality and the Self in Guidance: a Report on Three London Colleges*. Callander: Centre for Educational Policy and Management/National Association for Education Guidance for Adults.

Peavy, R.V. (1993) 'Envisioning the future: worklife and counselling', *Canadian Journal of Counselling*, 27 (2): 123–39.

Peck, J. (1996) *Work Place, the Social Regulation of Labor Markets*. New York: Guildford Press.

Pepper, S.C. (1942) *World Hypothesis: a Study in Evidence*. Berkeley, CA: University of California Press.

Pfeffer, N. and Coote, A. (1991) *Is Quality Good for You?* Social Policy Paper No. 5. London: Institute for Public Policy Research.

Piaget, J. (1954) *The Construction of Reality in the Child*. New York: Basic Books.

Piper, H. and Piper, J. (1998) '"Disaffected youth": a wicked issue, a worse label', *Youth & Policy*, 62: 32–43.

Pope, M.L. and Keen, T.R. (1981) *Personal Construct Psychology and Education*. London: Academic Press.

Popkewitz, T.S. (1991) *A Political Sociology of Educational Reform: Power/Knowledge in Teaching, Teacher Education, and Research*. New York: Teachers College Press.

Power, S. and Gewirtz, S. (1999) 'Reading Education Action Zones', paper presented to the British Educational Research Association Annual Conference, University of Sussex, September.

Public Attitude Surveys (1997) *Excluded Youths*. London.

Purcell, K. and Pitcher, J. (1996) *Great Expectations: the New Diversity of Graduate Skills and Aspirations*. Manchester: CSU.

Purcell, K., Pitcher, J. and Simm, C. (1999) *Working Out? Graduates' Early Experiences of the Labour Market*. Manchester: CSU.

QCA (1999) *Learning Outcomes from Careers Education and Guidance*. London: Qualifications & Curriculum Authority.

QCA (2000) *Disapplication of the National Curriculum* London: Qualifications and Curriculum Authority/DfEE.

Rajan, A., van Eupen, P. and Jaspers, A. (1997) *Britain's Flexible Labour Market: What Next?* Southborough: Centre for Research in Employment and Technology in Europe.

Rajan, A., van Eupen, P., Chapple, K. and Lane, D. (1999) *Employability: Bridging the Gap between Rhetoric and Reality. First Report: Employers Perspective*. Tonbridge: Centre for Research in Employment and Technology in Europe.

Rifkin, J. (1996) *The End of Work: the Decline of the Global Labor Force and the Dawn of the Post-Market Era*. New York: Putnam.

Roberts, K. (1968) 'The entry into employment: an approach to a general theory', *Sociological Review*, 16: 165–84.

Roberts, K. (1977) 'The social conditions, consequences and limitations of careers guidance', *British Journal of Guidance and Counselling*, 5 (1): 1–9.

Roberts, K. (1997) 'Prolonged transitions to uncertain destinations', *British Journal of Guidance and Counselling*, 25 (3): 345–60.

Roberts, K. (1981) 'The sociology of work entry and occupational choice', in A.G. Watts, D.E. Super and J. Kidd (eds), *Career Development in Britain*. Cambridge: Hobsons.

Roberts, K. (1994) *The Limitations of Guidance: Opportunity Structure Approach*. Vocational Choice and Development, Supplement 7.

Rodger, A. (1952) *The Seven Point Plan*. London: National Institute of Industrial Psychology.

Rogers, C. (1951) *Client Centred Therapy*. Boston: Houghton Mifflin.

Rogers, C. (1961) *On Becoming a Person*. London: Constable.

Rubery, J. and Wilkinson, F. (eds) (1994) *Employer Strategy and the Labour Market*. Oxford: Oxford University Press.

Sadovnik, A.R., Cookson, P.W. and Semel, S.F. (1994) *Exploring Education: an Introduction to the Foundation of Education*. Boston, London: Allyn & Brown.

Salomone, P.R. (1996) 'Tracing Super's theory of vocational development', *Journal of Career Development*, 2 (3): 167–84.

Savickas, M.L. (1993) 'Career counseling in the postmodern era', *Journal of Cognitive Psychotherapy*, 7 (3): 205–15.

Savickas, M. L. (1994) 'Fracture lines in career counselling', *NICEC Bulletin*, no. 42: 18–21. Cambridge: NICEC.

SCAA (1995) *Looking Forward: Careers Education and Guidance in the Curriculum* London: Schools Curriculum Assessment Authority.

SCAA (1996) *Skills for Choice*. London: Schools Curriculum Assessment Authority.

SCAGES (1993) 'Statement of principles and definitions', in C. Ball (ed.), *Guidance Matters*. Standing Conference of Associations for Guidance in Educational Settings. London: RSA.

Schon, D. (1991) *The Reflective Practitioner*. Aldershot: Arena.

Seligman, L. (1994) *Developmental Career Counseling and Assessment*, 2nd edn. Thousand Oaks, CA: Sage.

Sennet, R. (1998) *The Corrosion of Character: the Personal Consequences of Work in the New Capitalism*. New York: Norton.

SEU (1999) *Bridging the Gap: New Opportunities for 16–18 Year Olds Not in Education, Employment or Training*. Social Exclusion Unit. London: HMSO.

Smail, D. (1991) 'Toward a radical environmentalist psychology of help', *The Psychologist*, 2: 61–5.

Sonnenberg, D. (1997) 'The "new career" changes: understanding and managing anxiety', *British Journal of Guidance and Counselling*, 25 (4): 463–72.

Spivak, G. (1990) *The Post-Colonial Critic: Interviews, Strategies, Dialogues*, ed. S. Harasym. New York, London: Routledge.

Spokane, A. (1996) 'Holland's theory', in D. Brown and L. Brooks (eds), *Career Choice and Development*, 3rd edn. San Francisco: Jossey-Bass.

Stacey, L. and Mignot, P. (2000) 'The discourse of the careers guidance interview: from public policy to private practice', University of Reading, unpublished paper. National Youth Agency.

Sugarman, L. (1996) 'Narratives of theory and practice', in R. Woolfe and W. Dryden (eds), *Handbook of Counselling Psychology*. London: Sage.

Sullivan, E.V. (1990) *Critical Psychology and Pedagogy*. New York: Bergin & Garvey.

Super, D.E. (1957) *The Psychology of Careers*. New York: Harper Row.

Super, D.E. (1981) 'A developmental theory', in D. Montrose and C. Shinkman (eds), *Career Development in the 1980s*. Springfield, MA: Montrose.

Super, D.E. (1990) 'A life-span, life-space approach to career development', in D. Brown and L. Brooks (eds), *Career Choice and Development*, 2nd edn. San Francisco: Jossey-Bass.

Super, D. and Bachrach, P. (1957) *Scientific Careers and Vocational Development*. New York: Teachers College Press.

Super, D.E., Savickas, M.L. and Super, C.M. (1996) 'The life span, life space approach to careers', in D. Brown and L. Brooks (eds), *Career Choice and Development*, 3rd edn. San Francisco: Jossey-Bass.

Swanson, J.L. and Fouad, N.A (1999) *Career Theory and Practice*. London: Sage.

Tait, A. (1999) 'Face to face and at a distance: the mediation of guidance and counselling through new technologies', *British Journal of Guidance and Counselling*, 27 (1): 113–22.

Thompson, N. (1992) *Existentialism and Social Work*. Aldershot: Avebury.

Thompson, N. (1997) *Anti-Discriminatory Practice*. Basingstoke: Macmillan.

TUC (2000) *The Future of Work*. London: Trades Union Congress.

Turkle, S. (1996) *Life on the Screen*. London: Weidenfeld and Nicolson.

UDACE (1986) *The Challenge of Change*. Leicester: Unit for the Development of Adult Continuing Education.

Vandevelde, H. (2000) *Work Skills Resource Pack*. Richmond: Trotman.

Van Ments, M. (1994) *The Effective Use of Role Play: a Handbook for Teachers and Trainers*. New York: Nichols.

Vygotsky, L.S. (1978) *Mind in Society*, ed. M. Cole, V. John-Steiner, S. Scribner and E. Souberman. Cambridge, MA: Harvard University Press.

Watkins, C. and Savickas, M. (1990) 'Psychodynamic career counselling', in W. Walsh and S. Osipow (eds), *Career Counselling: Contemporary Topics in Vocational Psychology*. Hillsdale, NJ: Erlbaum.

Watkins, J. and Drury, L. (1994) *Positioning for the Unknown*. Bristol: University of Bristol/Clerical Medical.

Watson, T. (1987) *Sociology, Work and Industry*. London: Routledge.

Watts, A.G. (1983) *Education, Unemployment and the Future of Work*. Milton Keynes: Open University Press.

Watts, A.G. (1991) 'The impact of the "New Right": policy challenges confronting careers guidance in England and Wales', *British Journal of Guidance and Counselling*, 19 (3): 230–45.

Watts, A.G. (1996a) 'Careers guidance and public policy', in A.G. Watts, B. Law, J. Killeen, J. Kidd and R. Hawthorn (eds), *Rethinking Careers Education and Guidance: Theory, Policy, and Practice*. London: Routledge.

Watts, A.G. (1996b). 'Socio-political ideologies in guidance', in A.G. Watts, B. Law, J. Killeen, J. Kidd and R. Hawthorn (eds), *Rethinking Careers Education and Guidance: Theory, Policy, and Practice*. London: Routledge.

Watts, A.G. (1996c) 'Computers in guidance', in A.G. Watts, B. Law, J. Killeen, J. Kidd and R. Hawthorn (eds), *Rethinking Careers Education and Guidance: Theory, Policy, and Practice*. London: Routledge.

Watts, A.G. (1996d) *Careerquake: Policy Support for Self-Managed Careers*. Arguments 11. London: Demos.

Watts, A.G. (1999) *Reshaping Career Development for the 21st Century*. Derby: Centre for Guidance Studies.

Watts, A.G. and Hawthorn, R. (1992) *Careers Education and the Curriculum in Higher Education*. Cambridge: CRAC.

Watts, A.G. and Herr, E.L. (1976) 'Career(s) education in Britain and the USA: contrasts and common problems', *British Journal of Guidance and Counselling*, 4 (2): 129–42.

Watts, A.G., Law, B. and Fawcett, B. (1981) 'Some implications for guidance practice', in A.G. Watts, D. Super and J. Kidd (eds) *Career Development in Britain*. Cambridge: Hobsons.

Webster, C. (2000) 'Getting by: young people, transitions and social exclusion', paper presented to the conference on Research to Inform the Development of the Connexions Service, Department of Education and Employment, London, July.

Weick, K. (1996) 'Enactment and the boundaryless career', in M. Arthur and D. Rousseau (eds), *The Boundaryless Career*. New York: Oxford University Press.

Wijers, G. and Meijers, F. (1996) 'Careers guidance in the knowledge society', *British Journal of Guidance and Counselling*, 24 (2): 185–98.

Williamson, E. (1939) *How to Counsel Students*. New York: McGraw Hill.

Wrench, J. (1992) 'New vocationalism, old racism and the careers service', in P. Braham (ed.), *Racism and Anti Racism: Inequalities, Opportunities and Policies*. London: Sage.

Young, R.A. and Collin, A. (1988) 'Career development and hermeneutical inquiry. Part 1: The framework of a hermeneutical approach', *Canadian Journal of Counselling*, 22 (3): 153–61.

Young, R.A. and Collin, A. (eds) (1992) *Interpreting Career: Hermeneutical Studies of Lives in Context*. Westport, CT: Praeger.

Young, R.A., Valach, L. and Collin, A. (1996) 'A contextual explanation of careers', in D. Brown and L. Brooks (eds), *Career Choice and Development*, 3rd edn. San Francisco: Jossey-Bass.

Youth Justice Board (2000) *Mentoring for Young People at Risk and Young Offenders*. London: Crime Concern.

INDEX